THE FEW

A Call to the Road Less Traveled - The Call to Intimacy with God!

by David Mayorga

Published by

SHABAR PUBLICATIONS
www.shabarpublications.com

Most Shabar Publications products are available at special quantity discounts for bulk purchase for sales promotions, fund-raising and educational needs. For details, write Shabar Publications at mayorga1126@gmail.com.

THE FEW: A CALL TO THE ROAD LESS TRAVELED - THE CALL TO INTIMACY WITH GOD by David Mayorga

Published by Shabar Publications
3833 N. Taylor Rd.
Palmhurst, Texas 78573
www.shabarpublications.com
www.masterbuildertx.com

This book or parts thereof may not be reproduced in any form, stored in a retrieval system, or transmitted in any form by any means - electronic, mechanical, photocopy, recording, or otherwise - without prior written permission of the publisher, except as provided by United States of America copyright law.

Unless otherwise noted, all Scripture quotations are from the New Kings James Version of the Bible. Copyright@1979, 1980, 1982 by Thomas Nelsos, Inc., publishers. Used by permission.

Edited by Tania Joy Caballero

Copyright @ 2017 by David Mayorga
All rights reserved

ISBN 978-0-9991710-0-4

Table of Contents

FOREWORD 5

INTRODUCTION 7

PART I 11

CHAPTER 1: "I SAW THE LORD!" 12

CHAPTER 2: NO OTHER GREATER THAN THESE 24

CHAPTER 3: THERE IS MORE 30

CHAPTER 4: OBEDIENT TO HEAVENLY VISIONS 38

CHAPTER 5: I NO LONGER LIVE! 45

CHAPTER 6: HARNESSED BY THE LORD! 55

CHAPTER 7: LIVING IN ANOTHER WORLD 69

CHAPTER 8: BECOMING DIRECTORS OF HEAVEN
IN THE EARTH. 76

CHAPTER 9: FAITHFULNESS 82

CHAPTER 10: A HISTORY WITH GOD 94

PART II 105

CHAPTER 11: BE SOBER! 106

CHAPTER 12: "FATHER, I WANT MORE OF JESUS!" 117

CHAPTER 13: GOD'S HEART: TO HAVE THE PREEMINENCE 127

CHAPTER 14: THE OTHER SIDE 137

CHAPTER 15: I CAN'T WAIT TO FALL IN LOVE
WITH JESUS AGAIN! 147

CHAPTER16: OBEDIENCE GOES BEFORE THE BLESSING 158

CHAPTER 17: DECOGNIZING DOORS OF OPPORTUNITY 168

CHAPTER18: RENEWING OUR LIVES IN THE HOLY GHOST 178

CHAPTER 19: THE AWESOME FRAGRANCE OF JESUS 188

CHAPTER 20: THE KINGDOM IS NOT FOR
HALF-HEARTED PEOPLE 195

CHAPTER 21: THE MARKS OF A WILLING VESSEL 206

CHAPTER 22: TURNED INTO ANOTHER MAN 216

CHAPTER23: UNBELIEF BEING GOD'S GREATEST
OBSTACLE - PART 1 226

CHAPTER 24: UNBELIEF BEING GOD'S GREATEST
OBSTACLE - PART 2 236

CHAPTER 25: UNBELIEF BEING GOD'S GREATEST
OBSTACLE - PART 3 245

MINISTRY INFORMATION 255

MINISTRY RESOURCES 256

FOREWORD

I'm excited about this book. It's like sitting in a fine restaurant partaking of a deliciously prepared and presented meal. What a contrast to the Ramen noodle, macaroni and cheese meals we are accustomed to eating. While these microwave fast food type meals are better than nothing, they do very little to supply us with the nutrition our bodies really need. This book will not disappoint. It is jammed with more than enough spiritual nutrition to keep you going for years to come.

David is no newcomer to the ministry, having served for some twenty plus years as a pastor he is now heading up several Bible Schools where he is seeking to pour knowledge and experience into the lives of others. No, these are not your typical Bible Colleges with their fancy manicured campuses and lists of degreed faculty; but rather groups of students meeting on a weekly basis in several churches as well as one in Mexico.

To me this speaks volumes about the man and his mission. While he may not be a big shot in name recognition I believe, he is known in heaven and that is all that really matters in the end.

The prophet Elijah came on the scene stating, "As the Lord God of Israel lives before whom I stand." Elijah didn't claim to be a graduate

FOREWORD

of some Christian college or university but rather as one who stood in the presence of God. This book is written by a man who has spent time with God. Read it and I believe you will agree.

Now find a quiet place where you can draw aside from all distractions and enjoy feasting on this deliciously prepared and nutritionally healthy spiritual meal. You'll find yourself satisfied, and yet strangely enough, still hungering for more.

- David Ravenhill, Author & Teacher
Siloam Springs, Arkansas.

INTRODUCTION

It has been years that I have been carrying this burden in my heart for God's church and finally got the passion to put it in writing and share my heart with as many as would hunger for the same.
When I write or speak of "the few," I am in no way making or trying to demean believers who feel that they are part of "the few." Certainly, there are many who believe that they are following God to the best of their ability and without doubt are pursuing "the higher calling of God in Christ Jesus."

The type of believer that I call "the few" is one who has purposely aligned His heart with God's heart and daily pursues God's passion for his or her life and the purpose for which was called.

I think of Noah as one of my prime examples: God had something in His heart and needed a man that He could use to get this desire manifested. He chose Noah! Why Noah? Why not someone else in Noah's day?

Apparently, Noah had history with God and when God needed something done, He went with the one He knew and trusted. There is no doubt in my mind that Noah was part of "the few." Here's another example taught by Jesus in a parable:

INTRODUCTION

"Jesus spoke to them again in parables, saying: "The kingdom of heaven is like a king who prepared a wedding banquet for his son. 3He sent his servants to those who had been invited to the banquet to tell them to come, but they refused to come. "Then he sent some more servants and said, 'Tell those who have been invited that I have prepared my dinner: My oxen and fattened cattle have been butchered, and everything is ready. Come to the wedding banquet.' "But they paid no attention and went off—one to his field, another to his business. The rest seized his servants, mistreated them and killed them. The king was enraged. He sent his army and destroyed those murderers and burned their city. "Then he said to his servants, 'The wedding banquet is ready, but those I invited did not deserve to come. Go to the street corners and invite to the banquet anyone you find.' So the servants went out into the streets and gathered all the people they could find, the bad as well as the good, and the wedding hall was filled with guests. "But when the king came in to see the guests, he noticed a man there who was not wearing wedding clothes. 'Friend,' he asked, 'how did you get in here without wedding clothes?' The man was speechless. "Then the king told the attendants, 'Tie him hand and foot, and throw him outside, into the darkness, where there will be weeping and gnashing of teeth.' "For many are invited, but few are chosen." (Matthew 22:1-14)

INTRODUCTION

Just like many did not pay attention to the King when he was holding a banquet for his son, so it is today.

There has been a tremendous wave of lukewarm-ness come upon the believer today. What is of greater disappointment is that many believers accept it and feel no desire to "follow" Jesus with passion. What brings comfort to my spirit is the last line of these Scriptures: "For many are invited, but few are chosen." Who are the few? Those who chose HIM! Despite many not wanting to join "the few," God still has His servants who are in touch with Him.

Please understand that I'm in no way trying to be divisive in this writing though I am aware that some may think the contrary. My heart truly burns with desire for the body of Christ and the fulfillment of God's longings here on earth.

One of my prayers has been that through the writing of this book, many would be touched powerfully and become the ones that God uses to make a final push for the greatest harvest yet to come.

Yes, I do believe that God has special friends, and I do believe God has favorites. Who are these favorites? They are those who favor Him. Yes, they are those who have aligned themselves with God's passions to become "the few."

INTRODUCTION

In this writing, I have outlined some characteristics which I believe have tremendous potential to change your life if received with a spirit of teachable-ness and humility.

Allow the Holy Spirit to bring you to higher ground in Christ. While others pursue self-aggrandizement and self-fulfillment, apart from God's vision for restoration, you determine in your heart now to be part of "the few."

> - David Mayorga, Director of Masterbuilder Ministries, Inc. Palmhurst, Texas.

The Few

Part I

"For many are called, but few are chosen."
(Matthew 22:14)

1

I SAW THE LORD!

"In the year that King Uzziah died, I saw the Lord…" (Isaiah 6:1a)

One of the most powerful encounters that a man has had with God was recorded here in the book of Isaiah. It was so powerful that it shook this prophet to the core.

Many today are still experiencing visions and powerful encounters with God. Encounters like these have a tendency to leave a "mark" on you. They have the power to change your life and so much more. Those who desire to be part of "the few" must be able to see the Lord. Unless one has experienced the tremendous impact caused by God through a vision, dream, or some other type of personal encounter, the servant of God will be left wanting more.

Those who desire to be used by God must allow God to have His way in their lives – this would be the first principle.
Let us see what Isaiah saw:

"In the year that King Uzziah died, I saw the Lord sitting on a throne, high and lifted up, and the train of His robe filled the tem-

ple. Above it stood seraphim; each one had six wings: with two he covered his face, with two he covered his feet, and with two he flew. 3 And one cried to another and said:

> "Holy, holy, holy is the LORD of hosts;
> The whole earth is full of His glory!"

And the posts of the door were shaken by the voice of him who cried out, and the house was filled with smoke.
So I said:

> "Woe is me, for I am undone!
> Because I am a man of unclean lips,
> And I dwell in the midst of a people of unclean lips;
> For my eyes have seen the King,
> The LORD of hosts."

Then one of the seraphim flew to me, having in his hand a live coal which he had taken with the tongs from the altar. And he touched my mouth with it, and said:

> "Behold, this has touched your lips;
> Your iniquity is taken away,
> And your sin purged."

Also I heard the voice of the Lord, saying:

> "Whom shall I send,
> And who will go for Us?"
> Then I said, "Here am I! Send me."

(Isaiah 6:1-8)

There are three things that are vital for those who desire to be part of "the few" and we see them here in this portion of Scripture.

SEEING GOD

The first thing "the few" see is that they must see God. Seeing God transforms your life.

In some strange way, the revelation of seeing Him makes your spirit stand to attention. It brings eternity right down to mingle with your human spirit, and it quickens you with extraordinary "everything."

In other words, whatever was lacking in your natural being has now been imparted into you supernaturally. It's not like you turn into Superman but your faculties have been altered and now have the potential within you to align your life with God's.

MY OWN VISION OF GOD

I still clearly remember this experience as if it was last night: It was the Summer of 1989, after coming home from a Sunday evening service, that I began to feel a stirring in my spirit. I couldn't explain it but nevertheless it was there and it was real.

Up to that point in my life, I had been a believer for a few years and somewhat involved in my local church. I had decided that I would be a faithful follower of Jesus by trying to attend church as much as I could and if work would allow. I had also started paying my tithes and would occasionally attend a bible study held during Sunday school.

As far as Sunday evening church was concerned, I really didn't like going. After all, it was only a handful of people and apart from all looking like they wanted to fall asleep, it had the feeling like no one really cared to be there. Sarcasm? Hardly.

It was one of these services in which I attended with my wife -why I went, only God knows.

I still remember the preacher challenging the congregation to go and touch the world. He would express repeatedly, "Somebody has to touch the city, the nation, the world!" For some reason, I wasn't sleepy but truly felt something happening to me.

When the service was over, my wife asked if I wanted to go eat something. I told her I was not hungry, and she could tell I was upset. She asked if something was the matter to which I responded no. Yet deep inside I was being stirred, and I didn't know how to express it. I guess I was angry at something or someone. I know it wasn't at the preacher.

That same night I went to bed early because I needed to arise early and be at work by 7am. It was about 2am that I had this dream:

In this dream, I began to see myself standing on a street corner downtown McAllen. As I stood there, a Man (which in my dream was Jesus, the Lord) came up to me and asked me if I would mind walking with Him to the next block. I said, "Sure. I don't mind." As we arrived to the next block, He stopped and started to draw in the air. He made an invisible drawing of a building and asked me if I could see it. I said, "Yes." He then walked back with me to the place where He first met me. Then the dream ends.

I quickly awoke from my sleep and thought to myself how weird yet very real. After that, I couldn't fall asleep. All I thought about was the dream and what it could mean. After tossing and turning for a while, I decided to get up to pray.

As I prayed that early morning, I had a vision or something. Whether in the body or out of the body, I don't know. But in this vision, I see the whole east wall of my prayer room turn into a television screen and my dream re-appears on it. Wow! Talk about a giant screen television set!

In this vision, the very same thing that I saw in my dream replays itself on the screen, but this time, I'm the one viewing it as an outsider. I saw the replay with the exception that when I was taken back to the corner where Jesus met me, I heard a voice that said to me, "David, will you go for us?"

This voice was coming from somewhere. It was loud and clear in my spirit, and I knew it was the Lord. He was calling me to a life of devotion and separation for His glory.

I quickly responded to the voice with excuses: "Lord, I have so much hidden sin, and I'm not worthy!" The Lord said, "I will cleanse you." I replied, "I still have junk from the world hidden in places no one knows." He said, "I will take care of that." "Lord, I don't know very much of the Bible!" He said, "I will be your Teacher!" I finally said, "Lord, I don't want to go to other nations!" The Lord responded, "Just give me Your heart."

I wish I could say that I quickly jumped into the wagon to follow Jesus, but it took me about three hours to decide if I wanted to follow at this level.

I SAW THE LORD!

After having the Lord wait upon my reply, I said, "Yes, Jesus, take me and use me for your glory!"

It almost seemed like there was a host of angels around me waiting for this one reply and then it happened!

As I said YES to the Lord, quickly a kettle full of oil started to descend from the ceiling. This kettle lowered itself and stood about eight inches above my head and started tilting to be poured inside my head, not upon my head.

I began to tremble as the oil started to go inside my head. I fell to the ground with no strength whatsoever. When the oil finished pouring, the kettle went back up to the ceiling and disappeared.

I then proceeded to crawl out of the prayer room and made my way up to the bed. My wife had asked me where I had been. I said, "I don't know. I think I was with God." It was about 5am and almost time for me to get up for work.

After this experience happened to me, I knew something was different. I had a sense of destiny and the fire of God burning in me waiting to flow through me!

I share this experience with you for the sole purpose of sharing with you how seeing God and experiencing God will change you through and through.

SEEING YOURSELF

The second thing that you must see as "the few" is the ability to see yourself.

When you see yourself in the light of the presence of God, it will allow you to see how weak and needy you are for God and that apart from Him, you can't do anything.

Isaiah saw the Lord's glory first; then he saw his own sinfulness and need for God's cleaning power.

Without this second part to your vision of God, you will think that you are your own man and that you don't need anyone to help you get where you need to go. This breeds self-sufficiency – an unhealthy fruit of the flesh.

Also, one thing to notice here is that God wants us to understand our place in Him. He is God; He is first; He is the One who gives us the bright ideas for living, etc.

Why do so many disqualify themselves from forming part of "the few?" Usually believers disqualify themselves primarily because of the lack of humility. Humility basically means putting God first for everything.

Those who have walked with God understand that it's not by their own power that they accomplish God's work.

One of the things that one can see the need for when you see yourself in the light of God's presence is the need to be separated and consecrated to God. Those who walk in the company of "the few" are conscious of their associations and the world that surrounds them. They have an incredible inkling to sense God's presence and to know what He expects from them.

SEEING THE WORLD

The third thing that you must see as "the few" is the ability to see the world, the nations, and the lost.

First, Isaiah saw the Lord; secondly, he saw himself; and finally, he saw the need to go wherever God needed him to be.

As we see the Lord, our whole way of thinking begins to be altered to

God's ways of thinking. Sometimes we change quickly; other times we fight the Holy Spirit because of our rebellious tendencies.

I am thinking that Isaiah probably had a plan for his life already set and in motion when this encounter happened. Nevertheless, while contemplating the death of King Uzziah, something deep within his inner being brought him to attention and into the presence of God.

Have you ever been at this place? Things are changing around you, you feel lost and confused, yet while in spiritual hibernation God breaks in. Better yet, are you already doing what you think you should be doing and then God appears to change everything.

"The few" are servants of God who see, feel, and pursue the heartbeat of God and acclimate themselves to a heavenly realm. They are truly people who walk with the end in mind. Everything they do is with a kingdom mentality.

CHALLENGE YOURSELF and
GO DEEPER WITH JESUS in CHAPTER 1

1. Have you experienced God in such a way that it left a deep impression on you (a mark upon your heart)?
   If yes, can you remember how it happened and what it did in you?

2. Take time right now and evaluate your life before Him:
   - A. Do you sense that you have a healthy relationship with Jesus?
   - B. Do you sense God's holy fire upon your life?
   - C. Do you struggle with lukewarm-ness and a spirit of indifference?
   - D. Are you trusting God with everything in your life?
     - ☐ Your relationships
     - ☐ Your calling
     - ☐ Your business
     - ☐ Your family
     - ☐ Your finances

3. Are you presently walking in the revelation God gave you when you had your encounter with Him? If you are, that is awesome. If you are not, ask yourself why not?

- If not you, then who? If not now, then when?
- Be responsible with the revelation God gave you!

2

NO OTHER GREATER THAN THESE

"There are no other commandments greater than these." (Mark 12:31b)

"Jesus answered him, 'The first, of all the commandments is: 'Hear, O Israel, the LORD our God, the LORD is one. And you shall love the LORD your God with all your heart, with all your soul, with all your mind, and with all your strength.' This is the first commandment. And the second, like it, is this: 'You shall love your neighbor as yourself.' There is no other commandment greater than these." (Mark 12:29-31)

As you make your journey with God and have allowed yourself to be part of "the few," God will begin to show you His deepest secrets and desires. You will be soaring with God's passion.

What is interesting about the Ten Commandments is that Jesus said that the first two commandments were the greatest of all the rest. Apparently, Jesus knew something that other religious folk of His day didn't know.

The basic understanding that there is only One God and that we as created beings should love Him with all our heart, soul, mind, and strength. It truly is man's highest duty.

Loving God is more than going to church or doing a kind deed for someone. Loving God calls for a deeper, more intimate understanding of the person of Jesus.

The miracle of being born-again is that an open door to come into God's presence has been made available. Because of this access into the holiest of all by the blood of Jesus, you can come and discover all that God has for you, including the blessing of knowing Him more intimately.

THE FIRST COMMANDMENT

The first commandment takes a different turn within us as we allow it to pierce our souls and transform our minds in the secret place of prayer – just you and God alone.

Let me begin by saying that without the cultivation of a "quiet time" or time alone with God, the believer will find it hard to know God more intimately. Sure, experience teaches us so many things that are very important. Nevertheless, experience cannot and will not serve as a substitute for communion with God.

To love God with all your heart, soul, mind, and strength involves more than just a "mind" exercise or meditation of sorts. It takes more than just mere words to make it go into effect.

To cultivate any verse of the Bible and to make it practical and real, one must start with a confession of it. Right after your confession, the Spirit of God must make it real in us. Unless there is time allotted to any of God's truth in the secret place of prayer, the power of it will not touch your human spirit.

The goal of any truth in the Scripture is that it becomes part of who we are. We must allow the Word of God to transform our minds. We first make the decision to follow the Word; secondly it forms a behavior, then afterwards a habit, and then finally we start becoming what God desires for us to become.

Yes, to be "the few" is a little different than your typical follower of Jesus. In some big way, they are more responsible with detail.

THE SECOND COMMANDMENT

Every person that has ever spent much time with God has done great things for God. How can you not serve God with desire and passion when your whole being has been imbibed with God's glory in the secret place?

What I love about this experience with God is that the servant of Jesus, after spending quality time loving God with all his heart, mind, soul, and strength, is ready to explode into the earthly realm and cause a spiritual revolution among the hurting, the broken, and yes, the lost.

Great vision, passion, and desire will be birthed with the first commandment BUT great exploits are carried and manifested by those who enter the second commandment.

Yes, this type of follower is not only full of passion but of courage – they are called "the few."

LIVING IN TWO WORLDS

"The few" are as ordinary as the next person. What is special about these vessels of God is their desire to go the "extra mile" in everything they do. Yes, they are ordinary, but extra-ordinary in their desire to see God's kingdom manifested on earth.

These servants of God that I speak of are not content to just be in the secret place with God for the sake of saying they pray a lot - they are there with intention.

What is the intention? It's two-fold. Their intention is to be God's friend. They spend time in secret to hear God's secrets; then they arise and with intention go and impact their world.

Some are gifted in ministry, others in business. Yes, whatever their calling is, they know that the rhythm of heaven is concentrated on a "one-two" beat. That is to say - they pray as hard as they can as if everything depended upon God and they work as hard as if everything depended upon them.

They are not "religious" as many have faulted in our day. They have an eye in the secret place of prayer but they also have an eye in touching the world with the same glory they received when they were in the place of prayer.

CHALLENGE YOURSELF and
GO DEEPER WITH JESUS in CHAPTER 2

1. Has God ever shared His intimate secrets with you?

2. How is your personal life of prayer?
    A. Is it daily?
    B. Is it effective?
    C. Are you taking notes (journaling) of what God is showing you in His Word?
        - ☐ Make every effort to stay in daily prayer until you are clothed with power from on high. (Luke 24:49)

3. Are you asking God to reveal to you His heart for outreach ideas; the release of creativity for reaching the lost in your world?

4. Always remember to make your walk with God two-fold.
    A. Get to know the Lord in the most intimate way, by giving all your heart, soul, mind, and strength to Him.
    B. Take the Lord Jesus Christ with you everywhere and share His love with those who don't know Him.

3

THERE IS MORE

"We have not so much as heard whether there is a Holy Spirit." (Acts 19:2)

"And it happened, while Apollos was at Corinth, that Paul, having passed through the upper regions, came to Ephesus. And finding some disciples he said to them, "Did you receive the Holy Spirit when you believed?" So they said to him, "We have not so much as heard whether there is a Holy Spirit." And he said to them, "Into what then were you baptized?" So they said, "Into John's baptism." Then Paul said, "John indeed baptized with a baptism of repentance, saying to the people that they should believe on Him who would come after him, that is, on Christ Jesus." When they heard this, they were baptized in the name of the Lord Jesus. And when Paul had laid hands on them, the Holy Spirit came upon them, and they spoke with tongues and prophesied. Now the men were about twelve in all." (Acts 19:1-7)

IT'S LIKE CLIMBING A MOUNTAIN

To stop climbing a mountain when you know that there is yet more to climb before you get to the summit, should be a crime. Of course, unless you had originally made it your goal then it would be a great accomplishment.

Years ago, I read a story of how people would endeavor to climb the highest mountain in the world --Mount Everest reaching to about 29,029 feet above sea level. It talked about how climbers would make preparation and get ready for the big challenge.

Despite of all the fanfare and hype that surrounded these climbers, only a few make it halfway – not an easy challenge.

The article went on to say that by the time the climbers would reach the halfway mark, most of them, had lost their vision to get to the summit. They would conclude that the halfway point was better than nothing and would settle for mediocrity.

How many people in the kingdom of God have the same attitude when dealing with the things of God? When I say the "things" of God I am speaking of His eternal purpose and plan for us who believe.

OVERCOMING MEDIOCRITY

Mediocrity is a word that most people find themselves living. What is mediocrity? Mediocrity means to be average; halfway up the mountain; the middle of the road.

Many believers who could be and should be part of "the few" find themselves struggling with lesser things instead of pursuing the high calling of God in Christ Jesus.

Most outstanding servants of God are typical in their appearance but mighty in their resolve. They have a vision within which fuels their desires and passions to be productive world-changers and shakers for God.

When you talk to them about being hungry for Jesus, it doesn't mean the same thing that it does to others. For many, hunger means: "I read my Bible, go to church and even help when I'm needed."

In other words, hunger for some means doing what is expected but no more. True spiritual hunger means you crave the purpose of God to be done here on earth and you will not rest until you are moving towards it.

WE HAVE NOT SO MUCH AS HEARD?

The Scripture I used for this chapter speaks of the brothers in Ephesus. These believers were already moving in godliness and had accepted the baptism of John unto repentance but had never really entered the life of God. To them following Jesus was still an external thing until….

Yes, until the Apostle Paul showed up and taught them that there was more of God for them. They could have more of Jesus through the channel of His Spirit and so He prayed for their infilling. The rest is history.

I truly believe in my heart that many believers reach contentment way too soon. They stop climbing the mountain of God with the first obstacle that hits them. What is worse is that they have the gall to say, "The Lord told me to stop here." They conclude that that is as far as they are going to go and stop climbing.

THEN THERE WAS MOSES AND JOHN

To those who have dedicated your life to be ALL for God (to "the few") learn from the spiritual mountain climbers like Moses and John the Revelator. These vessels of God heard the call and climbed until they reached the summit of revelation and were transfigured by the glory of God.

"Then the LORD said to Moses, "Come up to Me on the mountain and be there; and I will give you tablets of stone, and the law and commandments which I have written, that you may teach them." (Exodus 24:12)

Is it enough to start a climb with God and not finish it? Absolutely not! You must remember that if God has extended the invitation for you to join Him on the venture of climbing to meet Him, know that there is a reason for it.

"The few" understand that going higher and deeper with God is the only way to satisfy this unquenchable hunger for more.

In the book of Revelation, the Apostle John had a similar experience: **"After these things I looked, and behold, a door standing open in heaven. And the first voice which I heard was like a trumpet speaking with me, saying, "Come up here, and I will show you things which must take place after this."** (Revelation 4:1)

This experience is the same as climbing the mountain to be with God, just like Moses did.

John saw a door open in heaven then a voice calling him to "come up here." How can John ignore that voice? Even if he wanted to pretend to be deaf, he wouldn't have been able to: It was too real; it was too powerful; yes, it was too convincing to be ignored. Apparently, the Lord wanted to "show [John] things which must take place…"

NO LONGER BUSINESS AS USUAL

Once you get yourself accustomed to moving by revelation or once you experience heavenly invitations, you will be "ruined" for ordinary Christian life. Going to church for the sake of just "showing your face" becomes tedious.

"The few" are no longer interested in pleasing man but God. They have seen "something" and that "something" has caught their spiritual eye.

They are living their lives to the beat of a different drum. Everything about them screams: "there has to be more than what I can feel, touch, see, taste, with my natural senses – there has to be more for me!"

What can we say about this type of passion? How can we explain it? Do we even attempt to try describing the spirit behind "the few?" My only explanation is that they have been impregnated by something from another world.

In the next chapter, we will continue to explore how these spiritual impregnations happen and how they have the power to transform a life.

CHALLENGE YOURSELF and GO DEEPER WITH JESUS in CHAPTER 3

1. Are you satisfied with your personal life at this present time?

2. Are you satisfied with what God has deposited into your life or do you hunger for more?

3. If you are not satisfied with the spiritual place you are to day, what are you doing to change that emotion of dissatisfaction?

4. Do you find yourself falling into mediocrity often?
    - ☐ Mediocrity means halfway up the mountain --in the middle of the road.

5. Do you find yourself starting new things and never completing them?

6. When was the last time you prayed, "God! Take me higher in my walk with you!"

4

OBEDIENT TO HEAVENLY VISIONS

"...I was not disobedient to the heavenly vision..." (Acts 26:19)

"As he journeyed he came near Damascus, and suddenly a light shone around him from heaven. Then he fell to the ground, and heard a voice saying to him, "Saul, Saul, why are you persecuting Me?" And he said, "Who are You, Lord?" (Acts 9:3-5)

INDEED, I MYSELF THOUGHT

During the encounter that Saul of Tarsus had on his way to Damascus, we see without a doubt that God had it all prepared. It was obvious that Saul of Tarsus was on a mission and perhaps was under the influence of an earthly vision.

Saul of Tarsus felt that his desires were pure and righteous and that this specific sentiment was a type of "green-light" if you will to cause havoc in the church of Jesus Christ.

Saul literally thought he was doing a good and honorable work by putting Christians in jail and beating them up. Listen to a man who is led by his own earthly vision:

"Indeed, I myself thought I must do many things contrary to the name of Jesus of Nazareth. This I also did in Jerusalem, and many of the saints I shut up in prison, having received authority from the chief priests; and when they were put to death, I cast my vote against them. And I punished them often in every synagogue and compelled them to blaspheme; and being exceedingly enraged against them, I persecuted them even to foreign cities." (Acts 26:9-11)

One of the dangers of earthly, fleshly, and/or carnal visions is that they usually are birthed out of selfishness only to produce selfish means.

Much of what we hear today in people saying that they have vision for this or that is nothing more than just an unsatisfied heart that needs "attention" – yes, much of it is a cry for the approval of others. Usually people who have selfish dreams and visions end up lonely, empty, and dry.

Saul was determined to move in his own strength and might to bring results which would look impressive to his contemporaries. His vision was without doubt a selfish one UNTIL Jesus showed up.

RECREATION

Another thing I must as well point out is this one principle: The principle of recreating with your hands what you lose in your soul. This is something that not everyone can discern at first, but eventually will live to see how empty it is to build something for sole purpose of pleasing self and not God.

"The few," in my opinion, are perhaps the sharpest most discerning when it comes to this one issue. Most believers would be content to do anything for Jesus – whether Jesus wants it built or not.

"The few" would differ in this area. They have truly made Psalms 127:1 their lives. Listen to this piece of heavenly counsel: "Unless the LORD builds the house, they labor in vain who build it; Unless the LORD guards the city, the watchman stays awake in vain." (Psalms 127:1)

There are builders who build because God has laid it upon their hearts; there are also those who build because of a sense of guilt. There is no intimacy with God – so the next best thing to do is to build for God something He will applaud. This is the trap of many believers. They run and run after the wind.

I truly believe God wants us to build, move, create and minister out of intimacy. "The few" are people who understand this principle.

KNOCKED-OFF FROM THE TOP

When the bright light hit Saul, and knocked him off his horse, he finally woke up. His whole earthly vision was overshadowed by a heavenly vision. I am not sure how long it takes for someone to meet God at this level or how far you must go living in stupor till God meets you, but this I know – when God does finally come - He comes!

When I think of those who are part of "the few," I can't but help to see that most of them have experienced God in a whole different level than your nominal or typical believer; this is what sets them apart.

It almost seems that they have been apprehended by a powerful conviction to go all out for Jesus. When they speak of obedience, for some odd reason, they are talking about obedience at a whole new level and a whole different understanding.

There is something about "the few" that sets them apart when speaking of following God. When they speak of following Jesus, it's more than just doing favors. For them following Jesus is all about disposition, willingness, and sacrifice. They truly believe that they know God in a deep way. They believe that nothing is impossible for them because God has touched them in some supernatural way and are now immersed in the glory and power.

Have you met servants of God with that deep conviction and assurance?

SPIRITUAL DISCERNMENT

One of the many characteristics I have found in "the few" is that they are people with incredible discernment. They can sense the moving of God like very few can. They can tell when the "cloud" is moving or staying and for how long.

They are constantly working hard at staying aligned with God and have such keen awareness to their surroundings. They see Jesus in everything.

It is one thing to have a heavenly vision, but it is another thing to acknowledge the Source where the vision came from.

Through heavenly vision, "the few" have discerned the wishes of God. Will you?

CHALLENGE YOURSELF and
GO DEEPER WITH JESUS in CHAPTER 4

1. Has God given you a picture or vision for your life? If He hasn't yet, He will. All you need to do is ask God to reveal Himself to you.

2. One of the keys to success in God is obedience. Once God reveals Himself to you in any way, shape, or form our next move would be to obey His immediate command. Have you moved with God's vision?

   - ☐ Many dreams and visions from the Lord die in the sea of unbelief.
   - ☐ Dreams and visions of God have died by the billions when the servant of God will not run with God's revelation.

3. Please note: When a person gets weary working for Jesus, it might be that He has been moving in the "flesh" rather than by God's grace and power. Evaluate and make sure that you are doing exactly what God wants from you.

4. Being busy for Jesus doesn't exactly mean that you are

moving in God's will for your life. Make sure that you are building for God's kingdom and not your own kingdom.

5

I NO LONGER LIVE!

"I have been crucified with Christ; it is no longer I who live, but Christ lives in me; and the life which I now live in the flesh I live by faith in the Son of God, who loved me and gave Himself for me." (Galatians 2:20)

As I ponder the subject of those who form "the few," I'm reminded of the Apostle Paul's great encounter with God on the road to Damascus. This was a time of revelation for Him.

Saul of Tarsus was not only knocked off his horse by the bright light; Saul met Jesus the King face to face.

What an encounter this must have been for this zealous Pharisee. What a powerful revelation of God's Son that was revealed to Saul of Tarsus. The encounter was so powerful that Saul was shaken to the core. Just listen to this:

"So he, trembling and astonished, said, "Lord, what do you want me to do?" (Acts 9:6)

There is no one that can say, "What do You want me to do?" - unless they have experience the miracle of the new birth with power. Saul did.

Is it any wonder that he penned some of the most powerful words of his ministry found in the book of Galatians? These words of devotion had and still stir the heart of the true follower of Jesus. If read "in the Spirit," they will go to the deepest parts, yes, to the spiritual marrow of our spiritual bone!

Let me attempt to unveil some of the secrets found in Galatians 2:20 as instruction for "the few."

These secrets are characteristics for those who truly believe that their lives are no longer their own; they have the revelation that they belong to Christ the King.

I HAVE BEEN CRUCIFIED WITH CHRIST AND I NO LONGER LIVE

The Apostle Paul begins this verse with these powerful words, **"I no longer live!"** It is of utmost importance to get this right; this fact must be established in the heart of every follower of Jesus. To be part of "the few," he must embrace the experience of the cross.

To come to grips with the realization that you are "dead to self" and "no longer live" can make all the difference in your walk with God. If you have a poor understanding of this fact, you will always struggle in your Christian walk. You will always feel that your walk with God is like climbing a mountain that is so high that it becomes unreachable.

Now, the servant of God who gets a hold of this truth will know that his life has been "set aside" willfully for the sake of God's life to come in and eventually come through.

"I no longer live" is a powerful statement one makes when the heart is overtaken by love, forgiveness, passion and desire for God. When the servant of Jesus understands this truth, he won't struggle with his or her identity any longer. When Christ comes in to rule, the servant knows very well, he must step aside and allow the King to have His rightful place.

BUT CHRIST LIVES IN ME

The other fact about Galatians 2:20 relates to the continuity of this experience. First, the experience, deals with dying; then with a transfer of life, God's life.

The fact that you died to self is the beginning of an awesome experience with God. As great as you might feel for coming to Christ and giving your life to Him, understand that this is just the beginning – there is more for you.

The "more" for you is found in this: "but Christ lives in me." As the servant allows God to come in with His life, a powerful transformation begins to take a hold of him.

An endue-ment of Christ's power will begin to download upon the servant's life along with the desire to please God in all things.

Another thing that the servant gets from God is His mind. The ability to think like God, to know what God is thinking all the time, is also given through the Spirit of God which is now working in him.

LIVING BY FAITH NOW

Perhaps one of the keys in this verse is the fact that when you died with Christ and He came into you by His Spirit, you also resurrected. You are no longer hanging on a cross, but walking in His power – resurrection power. You are now being led and directed to the works of God on the earth. You are resurrected and you are now a supernatural being.

Whatever Jesus did here on earth, where he was rejected, you can do also. You can move in supernatural power for the sake of demonstrating the kingdom of God in the earth. You can speak the truth of God with power and demonstration. The important thing here is to know that you are no longer dead but alive in Christ to do His work here on earth.

As part of "the few," you must realize that you have a responsibility to demonstrate what a resurrected person looks like in a very cold world.

TWO NATURES

Another important issue with being a servant of God, a part of "the few," is the mindset of duality.

In the times we are living, many believers struggle severely with overcoming. A world full of lust, sin, self and all forms of corruption seems to always bring them down.

Most of their Christian walk has been nothing more than a continual struggle to stay pure and focused on Jesus. Why is this? Why is it that they always look forward to a day without sinning? Their whole walk with Jesus has been a cycle of sinning and repenting, sinning and repenting, etc.

The way to overcome this vicious cycle in your walk is directly related with your mentality of how you see yourself.

Flesh vs. Spirit. Many believers see themselves living for Jesus with a life that is trapped in a body of sin. They see themselves hungry to sin, but knowing they are not allowed to.

One of the things you need to realize is that you have been set free from the law of sin and death. You are no longer in bondage to your flesh. Not anymore. Your flesh has been crucified to the cross and you are now living the life of another.

When one focuses on the flesh and the weaknesses that come from it, we begin making excuses of why we fall. We start saying things like, "I'm not perfect!" Or "I'm only human!" Or "We all sin!"

The minute you start saying to yourself: "I need to not sin! I need to not sin!" – it is when you do. Why? You fall into sin because you are trying to hold it back by using your own power.

It is when you realize that you don't have two natures, but one that you overcome. If you give attention to the selfish nature, it will get you! If you ignore it when he calls you and rather do what the Spirit of God desire from you, you will overcome.

The excuse we use by saying that we have two natures or dual natures has been such a stronghold on the servant of God. You had an old nature and that one was dealt with at the cross. You now have a new nature that, if obeyed, will bring glory to God.

AN INSTRUMENT FOR GOD

"And do not present your members as instruments of unrighteousness to sin, but present yourselves to God as being alive from the dead, and your members as instruments of righteousness to God." (Romans 6:13)

Those who belong to "the few" understand that they have been set apart to be an instrument for God. They have clarity of the purpose of why God saved them. They know that salvation through Jesus Christ is only the beginning of a life, which potentially, can make a difference in the whole world.

When one is born-again, he enters the life of God and God's life enters him. This alone sets you apart.

Living with the understanding that you have been set apart for God's use is what keeps you focused on the mission. When you allow sin to creep in and allow your flesh to dominate your thought patterns then you will find yourself fighting a war you can't win.

On the other hand, if the servant of God believes that he is now dead to self and alive from the dead to serve the living God, this one truth will forever change Him. He will now walk with knowledge and understanding of why He was born-again.

LIVING FOR HIM

"...and He died for all, that those who live should live no longer for themselves, but for Him who died for them and rose again." (1 Corinthians 5:15)

To be captured by John 3:16 and understanding the depth of God's love for lost humanity is as important as understanding 2 Corinthians 5:15 with powerful statement which says, **"those who live should no longer live for themselves...but for Him..."**

I truly believe that this one verse should be placed on every believer's heart. Those who belong to "the few" understand this one verse well. They have been consumed by God's presence and understand the importance of living for God.

To live for Him is more of a willful choice than anything else. Once you understand how the blood of Jesus has purchased you, you will discover the responsibility you have with the Master.

To be part of "the few" you must truly understand that you no longer live but Christ in you.

CHALLENGE YOURSELF and
GO DEEPER WITH JESUS in CHAPTER 5

1. After you came to Christ and surrendered to Him, did you make Jesus Lord of all?

2. Have you ever asked yourself the piercing question: "How 'saved' am I?"

3. Paul said, "I no longer live, but Christ lives in me." Does this portion of scripture bring about a great challenge to your spiritual life?

4. Since you believed in Christ and made Him your King:
    - ☐ Do you still set your affections on earthly things?
    - ☐ Do you still tempt God?
    - ☐ Do you still rob God?
    - ☐ Do you still long to run your own life instead of being governed by His Holy Spirit?

5. Have you have deliberately kissed the world goodbye with all its fleshly animations and foolish games forever?

6

HARNESSED BY THE LORD!

"Then Elijah passed by him and threw his mantle on him. And he left the oxen and ran after Elijah…" (1 Kings 19:19b-20a)

Why are "the few" called "the few?" Why are they distinguished by the parable as, "…many were invited, but only the few were chosen?" Why were they chosen? Why not others? Is God saying something in this parable to our hearts? Can you see it? Can you hear it? Can you perceive the heart of in all of this?

"The Few" are a people who see God in a different light and are attracted to His presence quickly. They have one goal in mind – to know Him.

As we continue our journey with "the few," it would be really a blessing to go deeper and see the motivation behind these vessels of God.

Let us see this one specific verse as we unfold the heart of why "the few" are such an attraction to God. I basically think humility is the reason for the attraction, but it's no mystery to know that God has touched them and now they want to touch Him.

POSSESSED BY JESUS

"I don't mean to say that I have already achieved these things or that I have already reached perfection. But I press on to possess that perfection for which Christ Jesus first possessed me." (Philippians 3:12 LB)

One of the most powerful combination of words which I have discovered in all the writings of the Apostle Paul are found right here: **"...I press on to possess that perfection for which Christ Jesus first possessed me..."**

To be part of "the few" you must realize God has impregnated you and now you are carrying in your spiritual womb something from heaven. You can't just sit around and "thank God" you're saved. You can't just go about your business as usual.

You can't just sit back and see the multitudes of souls in the valley of decision wandering in their stupor! No! It can't be done if God has possessed you!

God chased Paul and finally God caught him; it is now Paul chasing God. This is the very essence of one who is touched by God – all you want to do is touch God. Everything you do is with the intent to touch Him.

The same thing happened to a man of God in the Old Testament named Elisha. He was working, minding his own affairs, until Elijah showed up and threw his mantle on him.

THE PRICE OF FOLLOWING

"So he departed from there, and found Elisha the son of Shaphat, who was plowing with twelve yoke of oxen before him, and he was with the twelfth. Then Elijah passed by him and threw his mantle on him. And he left the oxen and ran after Elijah, and said, "Please let me kiss my father and my mother, and then I will follow you." And he said to him, "Go back again, for what have I done to you?" So Elisha turned back from him, and took a yoke of oxen and slaughtered them and boiled their flesh, using the oxen's equipment, and gave it to the people, and they ate. Then he arose and followed Elijah, and became his servant." (1 Kings 19:19-21)

Once Elisha experienced the mantle of God, he would no longer long to work the farm, to make money, or to please anyone for that matter. God touched Elisha. All he wanted now was God. All he wanted was his life to be engulfed by God. Is this your cry? Are you feeling the spiritual temperature of those who make up "the few?" It's no ordinary in any way.

Elisha sold everything that gave him his profit and embraced everything that made him a prophet.

He kissed his family good-bye and off he was to learn the ways of God, the ways of "the few."

When one is brought near in this manner unto God, it is with the purpose of harnessing. God is harnessing your life and is preparing you for greater use. Though you have been useful in the past, you are yet to find out your greatest potential as you allow your life to be harnessed by the Lord.

HARNESSED BY THE LORD

Have you ever heard the word "harness?" The word harness is defined as straps for animals. It is used to control the direction of an animal, i.e. horse or ox. So then to be "harnessed" by something or someone is to be directed and dealt by someone for greater purpose or usefulness.

If a horse is left alone and entrusted with his own ability to be productive, chances are, the horse will probably NOT be productive. It would probably waste all its time grazing or simply just be idle in the open field.

Since harnessing is an important thing to do if we want to see productivity, the Lord Himself also harnesses those he believes to be productive for His purposes.

He will reveal such a jealous love over you and will draw you near to His bosom. He will set you apart for training while others are still doing their own thing in their own way.

"The few" are servants of God who have been harnessed by God. God has gotten a hold of them and they are now only beating to the heartbeat of God. They have no desire to pursue their fleshly dreams or ambitions – they are done with pleasing "self" and are now captured by God's affections.

Years ago, I read a story written by Bill Britton. It truly impacted me in the deepest of ways and gave me plenty of understanding of how God prepares those who would later bring impact on earth. Here's the vision of Bill Britton:

"I Saw the King's Carriage"

On a dirt road in the middle of a wide field stood a beautiful carriage, something on the order of a stagecoach, but all edged in god, and with beautiful carvings. It was pulled by six large chestnut horses, two in the lead, two in the middle and two in the rear. But they were not moving, they were not pulling the carriage, and I wondered why.

Then I saw the driver underneath the carriage, on the ground on his back, just behind the last two horses' heels, working on something between the front wheels of the carriage.

I though, "My, he is in a dangerous place; for if one of those horses kicked or stepped back, they could kill him, or if they decided to go forward, or got frightened somehow, they would pull the carriage right over him." But he didn't seem afraid, for he knew that those horses were disciplined and would not move till he told them to move. The horses were not stamping their feet nor acting restless, and though there were bells on their feet, the bells were not tinkling. There were pom-poms on their harness over their heads, but the pom-poms were not moving. They were simply standing still and quiet, waiting for the voice of the Master.

There were Two Young Colts in the Field

As I watched the harnessed horses, I noticed two young colts coming out of the open field, and they approached the carriage and seemed to say to the horses:

"Come and play with us, we have many fine games, we will race with you, come catch us." And with that the colts kicked up their heels, flicked their tails and raced across the open field. But when they looked back and saw the horses were not following, they were puzzled. They knew nothing of harnesses, and could not understand why the horses did not want to play.

So, they called to them: "Why do you not race with us? Are you tired? Are you too weak? Do you not have strength to run? You are much too solemn, you need more joy in life." But the horses answered not a word, nor did they stamp their feet or toss their heads. But they stood, quiet and still, waiting for the voice of the Master.

Again, the colts called to them: "Why do you stand so in the hot sun? Come over here in the shade of this nice tree. See how green the grass is? You must be hungry, come and feed with us, it is so green and so good. You look thirsty, come drink of one of our many streams of cool clear water." But the horses answered them with not so much as a glance, but stood still, waiting for the command to go forward with the King.

Colts in the Master's Corral

And then the scene changed, and I saw lariat nooses fall around the necks of the two colts, and they were led off to the Master's corral for training and discipline. How sad they were as the lovely green fields disappeared, and they were put into the confinement of the Corral with its brown dirt and high fence. The colts ran from fence to fence, seeking freedom, but found that they were confined to this place of training. And then the Trainer began to work on them, with his Whip and His Bridle.

What a death for those who had been all their lives accustomed to such a freedom! They could not understand the reason for this torture, this terrible discipline. What great crime had they done to deserve this? Little did they know of the responsibility that was to be theirs when they had submitted to the discipline, learned to perfectly obey the Master, and finished their training. All they knew was that this processing was the most horrible thing they had known. Submission and Rebellion

One of the colts rebelled under the training, and said, "This is not for me. I like my freedom, my green hills, my flowing streams of fresh water. I will not take any more of this confinement, this terrible training." So, he found a way out, jumped the fence and ran happily back to the meadows of grass. And I was astonished that the Master let him go, and went not after him.

But He devoted His attention to the remaining colt. This colt, though he had the same opportunity to escape, decided to submit his own will, and learn the ways of the Master. And the training got harder than ever, but he was rapidly learning more and more how to obey the slightest wish of the Master, and to respond to even the quietness of His voice.

And I saw that had there been no training, no testing, there would have been neither submission nor rebellion from either of the colts.

For in the field they did not have the choice to rebel or submit, they were sinless in their innocence. But when brought to the place of testing and training and discipline, then was made manifest the obedience of one and the rebellion that lay hidden in the heart of the other. And though it seemed safer not to come to the place of discipline because of the risk of being found rebellious, yet I saw that without this there could be no sharing of His glory, no Sonship.

Into the Harness

Finally, this period of training was over. Was he now rewarded with his freedom, and sent back to the fields? Oh no. But a greater confinement than ever now took place, as a harness dropped about his shoulders. Now he found there was not even the freedom to run about the small corral, for in the harness he could only move where and when his Master spoke. And unless the Master spoke, he stood still.

The scene changed, and I saw the other colt standing on the side of a hill, nibbling at some grass. Then across the fields, down the road came the King's carriage, drawn by six horses. With amazement, he saw that in the lead, on the right side, was his brother colt, now made strong and mature on the good corn in the Master's stable. He saw the lovely pom-poms shaking in the wind, noticed the glittering gold bordered harness about his brother, heard the beautiful tinkling of the bells on his feet. and envy came into his heart.

Thus, he complained to himself: "Why has my brother been so honored, and I am neglected? They have not put bells on my feet, nor pom-poms on my head. The Master has not given me the wonderful responsibility of pulling His carriage, nor put about me the golden harness. Why have they chosen my brother instead of me?" And by the Spirit the answer came back to me as I watched.

"Because one submitted to the will and discipline of the Master, and one rebelled, thus has one been chosen and the other set aside."

A Famine in the Land

Then I saw a great drought sweep across the countryside, and the green grass became dead, dry, brown and brittle. The little streams of water dried up, stopped flowing, and there was only a small muddy puddle here and there.

I saw the little colt (I was amazed that it never seemed to grow or mature) as he ran here and there, across the fields looking for fresh streams and green pastures, finding none. Still he ran, seemingly in circles, always looking for something to feed his famished spirit. But there was a famine in the land, and the rich green pastures and flowing streams of yesterday were not to be had.

And one day the colt stood on the hillside on weak and wobbly legs, wondering where to go next to find food, and how to get strength to go. Seemed like there was no use, for good food and flowing streams were a thing of the past, and all the efforts to find more only taxed his waning strength. Suddenly he saw the King's carriage coming down the road, pulled by six great horses. And he saw his brother, fat and strong, muscles rippling, sleek and beautiful with much grooming.

His heart was amazed and perplexed, and he cried out: "My brother, where do you find the food to keep you strong and fat in these days of famine? I have run everywhere in my freedom, searching for food, and I find none. Where do you, in your awful confinement, find food in this time of drought? Tell me, please, for I must know!" And then the answer came back from a voice filled with victory and praise: "In my Master's House, there is a secret place in the confining limitations of His stables where He feeds me by His own hand, and His granaries never run empty, and His well never runs dry." And with this the Lord made me to know that in the day when people are weak and famished in their spirits in the time of spiritual famine, that those who have lost their own wills, and have come into the secret place of the Most High, into the utter confinement of His perfect will, shall have plenty of the corn of Heaven, and a never ending flow of fresh streams of revelation by His Spirit. Thus, the vision ended.

I believe that this vision is getting louder and louder each day. There is such a need for spiritual training in our midst. Most of what we hear has nothing to do with harnessing. Most messages deal with blessings and "get all you can from the Lord."

These types of messages as true as they may be (I agree we should all walk in blessing) we must move from spiritual adolescence to maturity.

We can't afford to stay spiritually retarded and/or lagging simply because we are selfish. Let us allow the Lord to drop on us His harness and allow Him to be our director, teacher and mentor.

CHALLENGE YOURSELF and
GO DEEPER WITH JESUS in CHAPTER 6

1. God touched Elijah then Elijah touched Elisha with the mantle (symbol of God's anointing and calling). Elisha gave everything up to follow Elijah (a type of Christ) and served him faithfully for 8 years or so till Elijah was taken up. In your own life, have you given up everything that might hinder you from God's high calling for your life?
   - ☐ An experience of God that cost nothing – does nothing.

2. Have you allowed the Lord to "harness" your life? Is He the One now in charge of your life, plans, and dreams?

3. Unless, God's faithful man is willing to be led by God, that man will never get to the place God wants him to be.
   - ☐ Are you trusting God with wisdom?
   - ☐ Are you trusting God with strength?
   - ☐ Are you trusting God with ability?
   - ☐ Are you trusting God with finances?

7

LIVING IN ANOTHER WORLD

"And I also say to you that you are Peter, and on this rock I will build My church, and the gates of Hades shall not prevail against it. And I will give you the keys of the kingdom of heaven, and whatever you bind on earth will be bound in heaven, and whatever you loose on earth will be loosed in heaven." (Matthew 16: 18, 19)

The Lord has promised keys to those who come to the knowledge of Him. It is obvious that God's plan is to equip a people who will learn the keys that bring forth breakthroughs in the earthly realm.

I believe that the heart of God is for powerful manifestations of His kingdom here on earth. Please understand that the manifestations I speak of are not in the realm of the supernatural though it may include them.

The manifestations that I am speaking of, relates to God's servant being obedient to God's heavenly plan and manifesting God's will here on earth. It is a manifestation birthed out of pure obedience to God's higher order.

ACCESS INTO THE REALM OF GOD

The first thing that "the few" have entered in to, is the very presence of God. Without entrance into God's presence, the servant of God will not be able to access anything from the Lord. "The few" know very well the great importance brought to them by the blood of Jesus.

"Therefore, brethren, having boldness to enter the Holiest by the blood of Jesus, by a new and living way which He consecrated for us, through the veil, that is, His flesh, and having a High Priest over the house of God, let us draw near with a true heart in full assurance of faith, having our hearts sprinkled from an evil conscience and our bodies washed with pure water..." (Hebrews 10:19-22)

To be able to connect with God, one must be able to come to God. As you enter into the "Holiest by the blood of Jesus, "you will be raptured by such great love and acceptance. "The few" know the power of access. They understand the power behind intimacy with God.

Access is the door, heart and mind of God. Access is only possible for those who have been washed in the blood of the Lamb.

Remember: Once you come in, you don't have to ever leave. You can abide in His presence forever! You can camp out in His presence until you want to. You can listen to God's heartbeat every single time He desires to do something. "The Few" have discovered this secret.

UNVEILING THE SECRETS

Most believers who have been brought into God's house know about God's Word (the knowledge about God's ultimate plan) but only "the few" know the secrets of God's heart.

"The secret of the LORD is with those who fear Him, and He will show them His covenant." (Psalms 27:14)

"The few" are a breed of servants who walk in the fear of the Lord and reserve their lives for His approval. In their relationship with God, they press in to please Him in all things – in return, the Lord reveals His covenant with them.

"Call to Me, and I will answer you, and show you great and mighty things, which you do not know." (Jeremiah 33:3)

One of the things that these servants of God go after are the mysteries which God has hidden and reserved for them – reserved only for those who dare "call" on Him.

When the servant of Christ purposes in His heart to love God and keep His words, a visitation from the Father is not far. God loves to dwell amid loving and obedient servants, yes, "the few!"

"Jesus answered, "If a person [really] loves Me, he will keep My word [obey My teaching]; and My Father will love him, and We will come to him and make Our home (abode, special dwelling place) with him." (John 14:23 AMP)

BRINGING A HEAVENLY INVASION

What about the secrets? What about the revelations and visitations that come from the Lord? Are they useful for something? Are they given only so we can "show off" and tell everyone how God speaks to us? By no means!

God chooses to reveal His heart to those who seek Him because He wants to impart some secret to them. I do not know all the secrets that God has in store for all of us, but one thing I know, every secret is given with the purpose of manifesting it here on earth.

Strategic information is continually being downloaded to the servant who cares to listen. The information from heaven usually relates to a strategy on how to impact earth for Jesus. It outlines methods on how to overcome darkness and take over its domain.

God is calling "the few" to a life of warfare; he is calling them to bring a heavenly invasion to earth – a possession of the land. Yes, the Lord is calling, and "the few" are stepping up to battle.

CHALLENGE YOURSELF and GO DEEPER WITH JESUS in CHAPTER 7

1. When God calls upon you to go higher by calling you into a fast for a season, or a deeper call to intimacy and prayer, it is God's intent to reveal to His servant some revelation about the servant's life. Once the Lord reveals to His servant things concerning his own life, the Lord proceeds to reveal His plan for him.

2. Have you felt God leading you into prayer and fasting?

3. Do you sense the Lord calling you to take a deeper look at His Word?

4. Are you being challenged to leave a life of normalcy behind? Why is This?
    - ☐ God wants to show you His world. It's an other world.
    - ☐ God wants to download a fresh touch of wisdom, power and favor upon your life.
    - ☐ There is a ministry that must be birthed for such a time as this and guess what? God needs your spiritual womb!

If you want God to have your spiritual womb, then pray…
"Oh God, here am I. Send me! Use me! Whatever you need from me, take it! It's yours! Whatever increases your kingdom in this earth – I want that!" Amen.

8

BECOMING DIRECTORS OF HEAVEN ON THE EARTH

"And the Lord answered me and said, Write the vision and engrave it so plainly upon tablets that everyone who passes may [be able to] read [it easily and quickly] as he hastens by. "For the vision is yet for an appointed time and it hastens to the end [fulfillment]; it will not deceive or disappoint. Though it tarry, wait [earnestly] for it, because it will surely come; it will not be behindhand on its appointed day." (Habakkuk 2:2, 3)

WALKING IN THE SPIRIT

One very interesting characteristic of "the few," is that they are believers who position themselves to be used by the Lord. They have one desire: to manifest kingdom principles in the earth.

This desire should be found in every born-again believer but the reality is that it is not. I'm sure there are reasons why some believers don't feel the burden of the Lord for His kingdom as others do, but the bottom line is that every born-gain believer must join the heart of God in touching the world with the good news of the kingdom of God.

To walk in the Spirit simply means that you are now living with heaven's blueprint at your disposal and will now make it your aim to manifest it. "The few" are servants of the Lord with one aim: to please God by following His instructions.

Walking in the Spirit is walking by God's desires, wishes, blueprint, leadership, instruction, revelation and vision.

To be able to direct for God heavenly principles on earth, the servant of God must be quick to hear, see and move to the beat of God.

EXERCISING THE MIND OF GOD

Once we know the rhythm of heaven and where God is leading, we must act upon what the Lord is saying to our lives.

You see, God is looking for someone that He can team-up with. He is looking for someone who will see what He sees, feel what He feels, and is willing to pay the price to see God's will be done on earth.

Exercising God's mind is putting into practice what God has so wonderfully released and placed in your spiritual womb. If you obey God's will, it will be manifested. If we don't obey, then we miss an opportunity of a lifetime to represent Him.

Believing is NOT enough!

I know many times you will get the brother or the sister who has visions from God and sees God moving and hiding behind every bush. Everything to them seems to be God speaking.

To as many as have revelatory gifts and do genuinely receive revelations from the Lord, I say this, "Believing is not enough!" There must be a transfer from the Lord into our brains and action should follow.

If no action is taken, the seed may be lost or the enemy might come and steal it from you. We must be quick to walk in the revelation of the Lord! Listen to this parable:

"Listen! Behold, a sower went out to sow. And it happened, as he sowed, that some seed fell by the wayside; and the birds of the air came and devoured it." And He said to them, "Do you not understand this parable? How then will you understand all the parables? The sower sows the word. And these are the ones by the wayside where the word is sown. When they hear, Satan comes immediately and takes away the word that was sown in their hearts." (Mark 4:3-4; 13-14)

DISCERNING HIS PLAN

The reality of the matter is that most believers are atrocious when it comes to discerning the plan and purpose of the Lord. They cannot discern the Holy Spirit revealing the Father's wishes.

Members of "the few" are people who dedicate themselves to knowing the seasons and times of the Lord. They are not living in "I-wish-land." They are people who have discerned the heart and intention of the Lord and are now working it out with fear and trembling.

"The Few" continue to be God's choice for the end time harvest. It's this breed of godly servants who will be rewarded handsomely by the Lord.

CHALLENGE YOURSELF and GO DEEPER WITH JESUS in CHAPTER 8

1. To "walk in the Spirit" basically means to bring your flesh under the government of God.
    - ☐ There are many things that hinder the flow of God in our lives. Here is my suggestion on how to overcome them:
        (1) Write them down (your sins, obstacles, personal struggles, etc.)
        (2) Confess them before the Lord one by one (in your own personal altar)
        (3) Rededicate your commitment to Jesus and His Lordship.
        (4) Walk in the Spirit (or in the wishes of the heavenly Father.)

2. Believing God when He speaks is just the beginning. When we begin to walk out what God has shown us then God's glory begins to flow.
    - ☐ Do you find it difficult to flow with God's direction?
    - ☐ Is fear holding you captive?

- ☐ Is doubt enslaving you to a life of mediocrity?
- ☐ Unbelief has left you wanting. Everybody is out of the boat and walking on water, but you are still inside of it.

3. Here's my philosophy for overcoming fear, doubt, and unbelief: You just do it!

9

FAITHFULNESS

"Moreover, it is [essentially] **required of stewards that a man should be found faithful** [proving himself worthy of trust]**."** (1 Corinthians 4:2)

One of the characteristics that I have discovered to be a bridge for those who would be great is a bridge I'd like to call: faithfulness. Those who form "the few" understand this bridge very well; it runs in their DNA.

Apparently, there has been much misunderstanding, on the part of believers, in the body of Christ in the subject of promotion. Some believers feel that just because they are in church and help or give offerings that this alone will get them some "brownie points" with God and His leadership.

Those who have aligned with the Lord and His calling understand very well that God is looking for a faithful bunch of servants who will hear and obey Him.

Why is faithfulness such a luxury in these times? Why does God choose the faithful over the gifted? Interesting point. Let us look at it.

WHAT DOES IT MEAN TO BE FAITHFUL?

In the Scripture I used above, it is clear what the Apostle Paul is trying to convey to any follower of Jesus.

If you have ever desired to be trusted by the Lord, then open your spiritual eyes to the many opportunities that God has made available to you. Every opportunity to serve the King is preparatory for promotion.

In the case that the servant of God fails in keeping with the Lord's command, will determine how much the servant can be trusted with future endeavors.

The word faithful means to be trustworthy, reliable. How many people do you know that have been irresponsible with the task at hand? Have you ever been to a place where the man who had the key to the door was not present? Everybody had to wait till the man with the key showed up to work.

In the things of God, one must be faithful in all things. You must be a man under God's authority, one who is governed by the Spirit of God and will yield to the smallest inclinations of God's heart.

If you ever think that God will use a man who has been unfaithful, you are terribly mistaken my friend. The minute a man "drops the ball" is the minute that his faithfulness is put in question.

God uses (what often appears as small and insignificant) exercises to discover how deep that faithfulness is. It may be as small as setting up chairs before a service, picking up some trash, or even making sure the restroom is clean.

If you have no eye for such matters, then God has no eye for you in kingdom matters. To the degree that you prove yourself faithful, is to the degree He will use you and trust you. Being faithful in public is a great thing, but faithfulness in private is even a greater thing.

We can do things for people to notice our work and yes, we might impress some with our long prayers and love offerings – but where is He that will stand in the middle of the battle when everyone else has given up and gone home?

DAVID'S FAITHFUL SOLDIER

In the story of David and his fall with Bathsheba, we discover how Bathsheba's husband Uriah was brought in from fighting against the enemies of Israel. Though David asked him to be with his wife, he said no to intimacy with his wife so that he might have intimacy with God (serving King David and pledging allegiance to Israel's army is like having intimacy with God).

Listen to this:
"Then David said to Uriah, "Go down to your house and wash your feet." So Uriah left the palace, and a gift from the king was sent after him. But Uriah slept at the entrance to the palace with all his master's servants and did not go down to his house. David was told, "Uriah did not go home." So he asked Uriah, "Haven't you just come from a military campaign? Why didn't you go home?" Uriah said to David, "The ark and Israel and Judah are staying in tents, and my commander Joab and my lord's men are camped in the open country. How could I go to my house to eat and drink and make love to my wife? As surely as you live, I will not do such a thing!" (2 Samuel 11:8-11)

PARABLE OF THE TALENTS
"

"For the kingdom of heaven is like a man traveling to a far country, who called his own servants and delivered his goods to them. And to one he gave five talents, to another two, and to another one, to each according to his own ability; and immediately he went on a journey. Then he who had received the five talents went and traded with them, and made another five talents. And likewise he who had received two gained two more also. But he who had received one went and dug in the ground, and hid his lord's money. After a long time the lord of those servants came and settled accounts with them.

"So he who had received five talents came and brought five other talents, saying, 'Lord, you delivered to me five talents; look, I have gained five more talents besides them.' His lord said to him, 'Well done, good and faithful servant; you were faithful over a few things, I will make you ruler over many things. Enter into the joy of your lord.' He also who had received two talents came and said, 'Lord, you delivered to me two talents; look, I have gained two more talents besides them.' His lord said to him, 'Well done, good and faithful servant; you have been faithful over a few things, I will make you ruler over many things. Enter into the joy of your lord.' "Then he who had received the one talent came and said, 'Lord, I knew you to be a hard man, reaping where you have not sown, and gathering where you have not scattered seed. And I was afraid, and went and hid your talent in the ground. Look, there you have what is yours.'

"But his lord answered and said to him, 'You wicked and lazy servant, you knew that I reap where I have not sown, and gather where I have not scattered seed. So you ought to have deposited my money with the bankers, and at my coming I would have received back my own with interest. So take the talent from him, and give it to him who has ten talents. 'For to everyone who has, more will be given, and he will have abundance; but from him who does not have, even what he has will be taken away. And cast the unprofitable servant into the outer darkness. There will be weeping and gnashing of teeth." (Matthew 25:14-30)

Some of the interesting points I have discovered from studying this parable have been how God goes about choosing how much to give to one and how much to give to another.

As you have observed throughout life, some people seem to be entrusted with so much; it makes us wonder why them and not us.

The Lord will always call us to Himself and entrust us something valuable to Him; something so precious to His heart will be deposited in our hearts then He will let us work with it.

Can we prove ourselves to be responsible and stay faithful to the original purpose that God designated for us?

To the degree that we prove ourselves faithful to Him, is to the degree that He will set His approval on future things. Many times, we get a "big break" to prove ourselves and we "drop the ball."

We can make excuses and try to prove our innocence yet God knows our hearts! It will all come out in "the wash."

It would be wise for us to know this heavenly fact: If we prove ourselves faithful with the two talents, God will double it up for us. If we prove ourselves unfaithful with the little - then know that whatever we have been given, will be taken away and given to someone who is being faithful.

WHEN WILL I GET PROMOTED?

> **"For exaltation comes neither from the east**
> **Nor from the west nor from the south.**
> **But God is the Judge:**
> **He puts down one,**
> **And exalts another."** (Psalms 75:6, 7)

Every form of promotion comes from the Lord (Man, leaders, pastors, bosses, fathers, mothers, husbands, etc.). It would make our lives less complicated if we would come to understand that they are all umbrellas in our lives AND to a large degree the channels that God uses to evaluate and consider if you're up for a promotion or not.

People want to be recognized and acknowledge for their great work, yet their attitude is wrong, their hearts are vicious being poisoned with jealousy and envy – God sees this!

Promotion always begins with submission. Attitude is everything in life. If you think you deserve a promotion, then you will not get one. If you humble yourself in the sight of God then chances are that you will flow with leadership. When leadership sees a genuine heart of kindness, then promotion is eminent.

We are to be responsible with our hearts. As you serve your immediate leaders and prove faithfulness to them, God will take special note of this.

However, it is that you treat your leader now, is how your followers will treat you later. We are only sowing for the other season.

LOYALTY: TAKING FAITHFULNESS TO THE NEXT LEVEL

If you ever really want to make an impact everywhere you go and with every person you meet, then take your faithfulness to the next level – BE LOYAL.

Loyalty is, in my opinion, the highway where the successful servants of Jesus flow. You see many people can show up to church at 10am and make their faithfulness be seen, but few will arrive at 9:45 am and make their loyalty known.

Loyalty is totally a heart issue. Nothing to do with a clock; it is more an issue with attitude.

WHAT IS LOYALTY?

"He who follows righteousness and mercy [loyalty] finds life, righteousness and honor." (Proverb 21:21)

Merriam-Websters Dictionary describes the word as follows: loy•al adjective [Middle French, from Old French leial, leel, from Latin legalis legal] 1531

    1.: unswerving in allegiance: as
        a: faithful in allegiance to one's lawful sovereign or government
        b: faithful to a private person to whom fidelity is due
        c: faithful to a cause, ideal, custom, institution, or product

Dear friends, to be loyal is the highest honor you can do for someone. Loyalty is not easily gained. There must be consistent faithfulness before you can realize how deep someone's loyalty really is.

So, when the ship is sinking and everyone is jumping off to save their lives, the "loyal" stick it out with you and help you bail water. Their motto is: "If we live, we live together; if we die, we die together!"

FAITHFULNESS

CHALLENGE YOURSELF and GO DEEPER WITH JESUS in CHAPTER 9

1. The word faithful in its simplest form means trustworthy or reliable.

2. It is required in stewardship for one to be faithful. What does this mean to you? (Write it down in your own words and meditate upon it.)

3. Evaluate your standard of faithfulness:
   - ☐ Do you keep your promises?
   - ☐ Do you show up when you say you are?

4. Have you proven yourself faithful with God's gifts and talents?

5. Have you ever been promoted because of your standard of faithfulness?

6. Do you know the difference between being faithful and being loyal?
   - ☐ If the activity starts at 10am, FAITHFUL people show up at 10am.

FAITHFULNESS

- If the activity starts at 10am, LOYAL people show up at 9:30am.

10

A HISTORY WITH GOD

"Then, when Mary came where Jesus was, and saw Him, she fell down at His feet, saying to Him, "Lord, if You had been here, my brother would not have died." Therefore, when Jesus saw her weeping, and the Jews who came with her weeping, He groaned in the spirit and was troubled. And He said, "Where have you laid him?" They said to Him, "Lord, come and see." Jesus wept. Then the Jews said, "See how He loved him!" And some of them said, "Could not this Man, who opened the eyes of the blind, also have kept this man from dying?" Then Jesus, again groaning in Himself, came to the tomb. It was a cave, and a stone lay against it. Jesus said, "Take away the stone." Martha, the sister of him who was dead, said to Him, "Lord, by this time there is a stench, for he has been dead four days." Jesus said to her, "Did I not say to you that if you would believe you would see the glory of God?" (John 11:32-41)

I have often wondered why Jesus was so moved with Mary's words and apparently not so moved with Martha's. They both said the same things, they both express their heart-felt sorrow for the loss of their brother, but only Mary's words made "Jesus groan in the spirit and was troubled."

Please do not misunderstand what I am saying - Martha also was trying to be spiritual about the whole matter. Apparently, she had been at some place where Jesus had spoken of the day of the resurrection. Martha, in her mind, believed that one day she would see her brother again.

"But Jesus said to her, 'Your brother will rise again.' Martha said to Him, "I know that he will rise again in the resurrection at the last day. Jesus said to her, 'I am the resurrection and the life. He who believes in Me, though he may die, he shall live. And whoever lives and believes in Me shall never die. Do you believe this?" (John 11:23-26)

Jesus was letting Martha know, *"There is no need to wait for the resurrection day! I am the Resurrection and the Life."* Jesus continues to pound this truth to a woman who apparently had developed little or never really cultivated any history with Jesus in the secret place of prayer. Jesus finishes Martha off by saying, **"Do you believe this?"**

I can think of the many times I have found myself begging for spiritual revelation regarding the matter of faith and total trust in Jesus. Have you been there? I do believe this word is prophetic and I am also certain that that which is coming upon your life in the next few months will be mightily affected by your understanding of this message.

First, I would like to place some needed attention to the groaning of Jesus. The Scripture says that when Mary fell at His feet broken and weeping over the death of her brother Lazarus, **"He groaned in the spirit and was troubled."**

Let us first, define this word groan or groaning. The word groan in Greek is brimaomai (to snort with anger) to have indignation on. Jesus obviously was so moved by Mary's weeping that He took it personally. Jesus was not about to let any devil get away with "beating-up" one of His children, especially those who are close to His heart, like Mary was. Hallelujah.

On the other hand, Martha seemed to be more concerned with doctrinal positions [hence her puny understanding of the day of resurrection]. Once again, let me make this issue clear: Doctrine without tears means nothing and does nothing. Martha was not lazy, don't misunderstand me, she was a servant of the Lord, but without brokenness consuming her being.

There are many believers today just like this woman Martha. She typifies the believer who is faithful to church, pay their tithes and gives huge offerings when the need arises. They even keep their doctrine to the "t", but don't know the heart of Jesus. They have never wept over their spiritual poverty, sin and "lifeless" Christianity!

These are believers who are possessed by a "Laodicean" spirit, a spirit that will characterize many believers at the end of the age. Just listen to these words:

"I know your works, that you are neither cold nor hot. I could wish you were cold or hot. So then, because you are lukewarm, and neither cold nor hot, I will vomit you out of My mouth. Because you say, 'I am rich, have become wealthy, and have need of nothing' — and do not know that you are wretched, miserable, poor, blind, and naked —blind, and naked." (Revelation 3:15-17)

I believe God loves all peoples the same, but I also do believe that God has "those" who are given to seek His face. There was a world of a difference [in weeping Christians] then; there has been a great difference today and there will be a great difference before Jesus comes to take His Bride away!

What separates believers today? Why is it that God pours out His gracious anointing on some and withholds it from others? This is something to seriously consider if we are to be part of that last day's remnant of God.

Before I share with you what God has been showing me regarding this awesome walk with the Lord, let us look intently at what gave Mary the favor with God as it has been clearly portrayed in John 11.

MARY'S HISTORY WITH GOD

"And she had a sister called Mary, who also sat at Jesus' feet and heard His word. But Martha was distracted with much serving." And Jesus answered and said to her, "Martha, Martha, you are worried and troubled about many things. But one thing is needed, and Mary has chosen that good part, which will not be taken away from her." (Luke 10:39-42)

"It was that Mary who anointed the Lord with fragrant oil and wiped His feet with her hair, whose brother Lazarus was sick." (John 11:2)

"Then Mary took a pound of very costly oil of spikenard, anointed the feet of Jesus, and wiped His feet with her hair. And the house was filled with the fragrance of the oil." (John 12:3)

I am fully convinced that Mary had abandoned herself totally to Jesus in full devotion and service. She had done things which nobody that walks in the flesh would dare of doing. She worshipped with total abandonment and gave herself and everything she owned away to the Master. She lived a life with no regrets, no reserves and no retreats. Are you?

The reason that Jesus was so moved by this godly saint should be of no secret to us. She had one life to live and she lived it for the glory of God. Her outward expressions of worship and service had been birthed in the deep corridors of her heart as she met with God day after day in sweet communion. She was not going to allow herself in no way to be hindered from living her life to the fullest for Jesus. She wasn't going to let no one set the pace for what she felt in her burning heart. She wasn't going to let Martha slow her down much less stop her from being at Jesus' feet; she wasn't going to let herself be intimidated or detoured from the wicked Judas Iscariot (see John 12:1-6)

Oh! to God, this woman was heaven-bound! She had known God in secret and now was not only ready to express Him to the whole world but was going to spend her most costly thing that she ever owned on Him: **"Then Mary took a pound of very costly oil of spikenard, anointed the feet of Jesus."** (John 12:3a)

Oh Church, please listen to the expressed-biblical pattern of Christian devotion unto God. You get to know Him in secret first, after that you portray or express Him – publicly. Amen.

So how do we make this history with God? How do we avail ourselves of Mary's secret? "The few" have discovered the secret.

REQUIREMENTS TO FIND FAVOR WITH GOD

You must be "poor in spirit."

"Blessed are the poor in spirit, for theirs is the kingdom of heaven." (Matthew 5:3)

The Scripture expressly teaches us that those who possess kingdom of heaven riches, practice poverty of spirit. What is poverty of spirit? Poverty of spirit has nothing to do with your bank account or anything material, it has to do with an attitude of need, yes, the need for God.

Unless there is an attitude of contriteness and humility of heart, there will never be any favor from the Lord on your behalf. Listen to Isaiah the prophet:

"But on this one will I look: On him who is poor and of a contrite spirit." (Isaiah 66:2)

This message puts a damper on all the wicked preaching and teaching of evangelical humanism.

You must have a ready spirit of obedience. A true servant of Jesus must be quick to hear and quick to obey Him! Things happen when a servant of the Lord obeys God's written Word. Miracles happen when a servant of the Lord also obeys God's prophetic Word. Listen to this:

"Now it happened as He went to Jerusalem that He passed through the midst of Samaria and Galilee. Then as He entered a certain village, there met Him ten men who were lepers, who stood afar off. And they lifted up their voices and said, "Jesus, Master, have mercy on us!" So when He saw them, He said to them, "Go, show yourselves to the priests." And so it was that as they went, they were cleansed." (Luke 17:11-14)

Always remember, the only reason that God speaks to You is to bring some result that will bring Him all the glory.

You must have a heart that abounds in thanksgiving unto the Lord.

One of the things that many servants of the Lord have lost is to give thanks to God for their calling. I as a servant can truly say that I didn't deserve this awesome calling. My wicked selfish life disqualified me totally from serving my King. Jesus saw something different – He believed in me. Paul put it this way:

"And I thank Christ Jesus our Lord who has enabled me, because He counted me faithful, putting me into the ministry, although I was formerly a blasphemer, a persecutor, and an insolent man; but I obtained mercy because I did it ignorantly in unbelief. And the grace of our Lord was exceedingly abundant, with faith and love which are in Christ Jesus." (1Timothy 1:12-14)

Dear saints of God, let us cultivate a history with God – one day we will reap the fruit of it.

CHALLENGE YOURSELF and GO DEEPER WITH JESUS in CHAPTER 10

1. Does God know you as an intimate friend OR is He just an acquaintance of yours?

2. Can you tell in your own spirit when God is far from you?

3. Can you tell the difference of when He is upon you and when He is not?

4. Do you sense you get God's attention when you call upon Him?

Secrets of How to Become Intimate with God

- Arise early (preferably before dawn) and seek God's face in prayer.

- Worship, give Him thanks, confess your sins, intercede and make your petitions known.

- Open your heart and express yourself to God holding nothing back.

- ☐ Read the Word of God (I recommend a year Bible reading plan)

- ☐ As you read, meditate on what you are reading (in other words, chew it and chew it, and chew it until it makes sense to your spirit)

- ☐ Write down (in a personal journal) what God is telling you during your meditation of God's Word. [Make sure to date your entry.]

- ☐ Commit your life to God for that day.

[Add-On's to Your Spiritual Practices]

- ☐ Taking a personal Lord's Supper on your own after prayer.

- ☐ Fasting for the day.

The Few

Part II

"After these things I looked, and behold, a door standing open in heaven. And the first voice which I heard was like a trumpet speaking with me, saying, "Come up here, and I will show you things which must take place after this."

(Revelation 4:1)

11

BE SOBER!

"But concerning the times and the seasons, brethren, you have no need that I should write to you. For you yourselves know perfectly that the day of the Lord so comes as a thief in the night. For when they say, "Peace and safety!" then sudden destruction comes upon them, as labor pains upon a pregnant woman. And they shall not escape. But you, brethren, are not in darkness, so that this Day should overtake you as a thief. You are all sons of light and sons of the day. We are not of the night nor of darkness. Therefore, let us not sleep, as others do, but let us watch and be sober. For those who sleep, sleep at night, and those who get drunk are drunk at night. But let us who are of the day be sober, putting on the breastplate of faith and love, and as a helmet the hope of salvation. For God did not appoint us to wrath, but to obtain salvation through our Lord Jesus Christ, who died for us, that whether we wake or sleep, we should live together with Him. Therefore comfort each other and edify one another, just as you also are doing." (1 (Thessalonians 5:1-11)

"Therefore gird up the loins of your mind, be sober, and rest your hope fully upon the grace that is to be brought to you at the revelation of Jesus Christ; as obedient children, not conforming yourselves to the former lusts, as in your ignorance; but as He who called you is holy, you also be holy in all your conduct, because it is written, "Be holy, for I am holy." (1 Peter 1:13-16)

"Be sober, be vigilant; because your adversary the devil walks about like a roaring lion, seeking whom he may devour. Resist him, steadfast in the faith, knowing that the same sufferings are experienced by your brotherhood in the world. But may the God of all grace, who called us to His eternal glory by Christ Jesus, after you have suffered a while, perfect, establish, strengthen, and settle you. To Him be the glory and the dominion forever and ever. Amen." (1 Peter 5:8-11)

Another powerful principle I have seen in this company that I call "the few" is how important it is to always remain sober.

The word sober, as used in the Scriptures above, means - nepho (nay'-fo) - to abstain from wine (keep sober), i.e. (figuratively) be discreet: be sober, watch. The picture we get from this word is far beyond being sober regarding drunkenness.

It is a soberness teamed up with watchfulness. To be sober means to watch; to stay alert; to stay awake. It means to not be drunk regarding wine but also to not be drunk with the world – or the spirit of the world. The wine that the world offers is truly intoxicating. It makes people lose their way. It makes even the very elect of God to fall into such drunkenness that they abandon the will of God. Paul admonishes us when He says, **"Therefore do not be unwise, but understand what the will of the Lord is. And do not be drunk with wine, in which is dissipation; but be filled with the Spirit…"** (Ephesians 5:17-18)

When a vessel of the Lord begins to get drunk with the world, and forsakes the command of the Lord to be sober, destruction is eminent. This marks the beginning of sorrow for such a one. Spiritual drunkenness is marked by one major characteristic – the abandoning of the will of God. Once flesh begins to take over, every decision made (no matter how good the intention is,) is on the path of death! If there is anything worse than natural drunkenness is spiritual drunkenness. Just listen:

"Wine is a mocker, strong drink is a brawler, and whoever is led astray by it is not wise." (Proverbs 20:1)

"Who has woe? Who has sorrow? Who has contentions? Who has complaints? Who has wounds without cause? Who has redness of eyes? Those who linger long at the wine, those who go in search

of mixed wine. Do not look on the wine when it is red, when it sparkles in the cup, when it swirls around smoothly; At the last it bites like a serpent, and stings like a viper."** (Proverbs 23:29-32)

Spiritual drunkenness is one of the greatest weapons that Satan has unleashed in these last days. It is in the fiber of our society. It consumes believers with a mirage. Its delusion seems so real but in the end, it will kill you.

OUR ADVERSARY, A ROARING LION?

"Be sober, be vigilant; because your adversary the devil walks about like a roaring lion, seeking whom he may devour." (1 Peter 5:8)

As a young believer, I used to always wonder about this passage. One thing was clear to me – the devil was not playing games with me. I also thought to myself, "If the devil is like a roaring lion and he wants to devour me, why does he want to do this? Why would the devil want to devour a simple believer like me? What have I done?" It wasn't long before I came to the reality of this verse and started to walk soberly before the Lord.

I discovered a few things about the devil and his dirty works. I realized that he was very interested in turning the work that God had done in me into nothing. The thing that the devil wanted to devour was the will of God in me; his whole goal has been to detour me from what God had and has in store for my life.

NEHEMIAH STIRRED BY THE WILL OF GOD

"The words of Nehemiah the son of Hachaliah. It came to pass in the month of Chislev, in the twentieth year, as I was in Shushan the citadel, that Hanani one of my brethren came with men from Judah; and I asked them concerning the Jews who had escaped, who had survived the captivity, and concerning Jerusalem. And they said to me, **"The survivors who are left from the captivity in the province are there in great distress and reproach. The wall of Jerusalem is also broken down, and its gates are burned with fire. So it was, when I heard these words, that I sat down and wept, and mourned for many days; I was fasting and praying before the God of heaven."** (Nehemiah 1:1-4)

Nehemiah, the servant of God was serving the King of Persia in the palace as a cup-bearer when some of his friends came to visit him. This visit was no ordinary visit for the Lord had other things in mind for Nehemiah. It was to be a day of destiny for this man.

His friends brought word concerning the Jews who had escaped and survived the captivity and regarding Jerusalem. Normally, our hearts would be filled with sympathy to hear bad new regarding people we know - this was different. Nehemiah was not only filled with sadness, but **"...sat down and wept, and mourned for many days..."**

Nehemiah was moved by the Holy Ghost to enter into another dimension, the dimension of God. He felt moved by the Lord to do something about the "distress and reproach" that had come upon God's people.

Any man who sets himself to restore or rebuild God's kingdom will always be confronted by the devil. Any man or woman of God who determines in their heart to do all the will of God will be confronted with such fury from Satan. My question to you is, "Are you ready to face hell?"

NEHEMIAH'S ENEMIES

As we have been dealing with being sober in the Lord, you might wonder what Nehemiah has anything to do with being spiritually sober? Nehemiah typifies the last army days in many different applications, but nothing depicts the enemy in the last days more than

Nehemiah's three enemies.

After Nehemiah came to Jerusalem and evaluated the damage of battle, he spoke to his group:

"Then I said to them, "You see the distress that we are in, how Jerusalem lies waste, and its gates are burned with fire. Come and let us build the wall of Jerusalem, that we may no longer be a reproach." And I told them of the hand of my God which had been good upon me, and also of the king's words that he had spoken to me. So they said, "Let us rise up and build." Then they set their hands to this good work. But when Sanballat the Horonite, Tobiah the Ammonite official, and Geshem the Arab heard of it, they laughed at us and despised us, and said, "What is this thing that you are doing? Will you rebel against the king?" So I answered them, and said to them, "The God of heaven Himself will prosper us; therefore we His servants will arise and build, but you have no heritage or right or memorial in Jerusalem." (Nehemiah 2:17-20)

Nehemiah was immediately confronted with his enemies Sanballat, Tobiah and Geshem. They had no interest in rebuilding the city of the great king. They had ill-will towards anything godly and holy. They were determined to stop the work at any cost.

Dear ones, doesn't this sound like Satan all over again? Doesn't this sound like the enemy who is trying to hinder God's work in the last day - both in personal and corporate levels? But how does he do it?

NEHEMIAH REMAINS SOBER AND VIGILANT

At the close of the project, the enemy once again comes and tries to hinder the work one last time, how did he do it? Amazingly, it wasn't by force or intimidation! It was done through deceit. The devil once again aims at the alertness of Nehemiah. The same is going on today! How is the alertness of the believer? Are we alert? Are we sober? Or are we too drunk with wine from the world that we can't discern the voice of God? Let us see our example:

"Now it happened when Sanballat, Tobiah, Geshem the Arab, and the rest of our enemies heard that I had rebuilt the wall, and that there were no breaks left in it (though at that time I had not hung the doors in the gates), that Sanballat and Geshem sent to me, saying, "Come, let us meet together among the villages in the plain of Ono." But they thought to do me harm. So I sent messengers to them, saying, "I am doing a great work, so that I cannot come down. Why should the work cease while I leave it and go down to you?" But they sent me this message four times, and I answered them in the same manner." (Nehemiah 6:1-4)

BE SOBER!

Nehemiah didn't entertain the enemies voice, oh no. Nehemiah was sober, he was alert and He said, **"I am doing a great work, so that I cannot come down. Why should the work cease while I leave it and go down to you?"**

I strongly believe that this should be our reply every time the devil comes to take us away from God's will. We should be so sober, so focused that we do not fall for his lies.

Remember the devil's plan has been in play since the beginning of your salvation to devour you by way of taking you totally out of the will of God. May we remain sober and vigilant. Selah.

BE SOBER!

CHALLENGE YOURSELF and GO DEEPER WITH JESUS in CHAPTER 11

1. Have you experienced the temptation of leaving your commitment to serving Jesus behind simply because you were discouraged?

2. The enemy would love to come after you and bring you down if you fall asleep (spiritually speaking). What things can you do to stay alert and watchful in the Lord?
    a. _____
    b. _____
    c. _____
    d. _____
    e. _____

3. Nehemiah was one of God's greatest reformers – he rebuilt the walls of Jerusalem and brought order back to a nation. All this came at a very high cost. Are you willing to pay the cost to have God use you to the maximum?

4. We all have enemies that make every effort to destroy God's vision in our hearts? Can you list your

enemies and begin to pray for God to undo the enemy's work in your life, family and ministry?

12

"FATHER, I WANT MORE OF JESUS!"

"That I may know Him and the power of His resurrection, and the fellowship of His sufferings, being conformed to His death..." (Philippians 3:10)

When I first read this portion of Scripture, I came to realize that the Apostle Paul still hungered for more of Jesus. This great man of God had already been to heaven and seen the Lord. This man of God had already begun in the work of church planting the establishment of leaders in various churches. What more could a servant of the Lord ask for?

I find that the Apostle Paul was a man who longed to know God. It burned in his inner man to go deeper into the beauty of Christ. I believe that sometimes we as believers reach certain "mile-stones" and become content with the outcome of a specific blessing. Now, the few, are a different breed. They know that there is more of Jesus to be gained.

Paul was no more different than You and I for he was also human; but he had a hunger to know Jesus more and more! We, too often get satisfied with the "tiny morsel" of some good work and don't press in to the deeper walk with Jesus. We become content with an outward thing and don't press in into His beauty.

Now not all believers are satisfied with what they have attained in Christ. There are many believers who have a genuine hunger for more of Jesus. They thirst and hunger for righteousness and their inner man screams to behold their Maker and their King!

If you have offered this prayer just recently or maybe ten or twenty years ago, then get ready for the fire of God to come down upon your life and transform you!

A HOLY FIRE!

"Now the glory of the LORD rested on Mount Sinai, and the cloud covered it six days. And on the seventh day He called to Moses out of the midst of the cloud. The sight of the glory of the LORD was like a consuming fire on the top of the mountain in the eyes of the children of Israel. So Moses went into the midst of the cloud and went up into the mountain. And Moses was on the mountain forty days and forty nights." (Exodus 24:16-18)

"For our God is a consuming fire." (Hebrews 12:29)

"The LORD reigns; Let the earth rejoice; Let the multitude of isles be glad! Clouds and darkness surround Him; righteousness and justice are the foundation of His throne. A fire goes before Him, and burns up His enemies round about." (Psalm 97:1-3)

It is evident by looking at the Scriptures, that the Lord is a consuming fire. His glory is a consuming fire and obviously, a fire goes before Him. Too often believers without knowing, they offer a prayer to the Lord as the one mentioned as a title here. They long to know Jesus more! The only thing that they don't know is that "a fire" of God's glory surrounds Him. So as you get closer to God, the hotter it gets! Have you found that to be so? It is the Lord's consuming fire! Fire is used by goldsmith to purify the gold and make it useful. It is the fire that brings out the beauty in gold. When one prays, "God let me see You," the believer is really inviting himself to a fiery furnace of God's presence. Amen.

THE FURNACE OF AFFLICTION: GOD'S ORDER FOR REVELATION

"Therefore at that time certain Chaldeans came forward and accused the Jews. They spoke and said to King Nebuchadnezzar, 'O king, live forever! You, O king, have made a decree that everyone who hears the sound of the horn, flute, harp, lyre, and psaltery, in symphony with all kinds of music, shall fall down and worship the gold image; and whoever does not fall down and worship shall be cast into the midst of a burning fiery furnace. There are certain Jews whom you have set over the affairs of the province of Babylon: Shadrach, Meshach, and Abed-Nego; these men, O king, have not paid due regard to you. They do not serve your gods or worship the gold image which you have set up.' Then Nebuchadnezzar, in rage and fury, gave the command to bring Shadrach, Meshach, and Abed-Nego. So they brought these men before the king. Nebuchadnezzar spoke, saying to them, "Is it true, Shadrach, Meshach, and Abed-Nego, that you do not serve my gods or worship the gold image which I have set up? Now if you are ready at the time you hear the sound of the horn, flute, harp, lyre, and psaltery, in symphony with all kinds of music, and you fall down and worship the image which I have made, good! But if you do not worship, you shall be cast immediately into the midst of a burning fiery furnace. And who is the god who will deliver you from my hands?" Shadrach, Meshach, and Abed-Nego answered and said to the king, "O Nebuchadnezzar, we have no need to answer you in this matter. If that is the case, our God whom we serve is able to deliver us from the burning fiery furnace, and He will deliver us from your hand, O king. But if not, let it be known to you, O king, that we do not serve your gods, nor will we worship the gold image which you have set up." Then Nebuchadnezzar was full of fury, and the expression on his face changed toward Shadrach, Meshach, and Abed-Nego. He spoke and commanded that they heat the furnace seven times more than it was usually heated. And he commanded certain mighty men of valor who were in his army to bind Shadrach, Meshach, and Abed-Nego, and cast them into the burning fiery furnace. Then these men were bound in their coats, their trousers, their turbans, and their other garments, and were cast into the midst of the burning fiery furnace. Therefore, because the king's command was urgent, and the furnace exceedingly hot, the flame of the fire killed those men who took up Shadrach, Meshach, and Abed-Nego. And these three men, Shadrach, Meshach, and Abed-Nego, fell down bound into the midst of the burning fiery furnace. Then King Nebuchadnezzar was astonished; and he rose in haste and spoke, saying to his counselors, "Did we not cast three men bound into the midst of the fire?" They answered and said to the king, "True, O king." "Look!" he answered, "I see four men loose, walking in the midst of the fire; and they are not hurt, and the form of the fourth is like the Son of God." (Daniel 3:8-25)

The story mentioned above regarding the three Jewish young men, has to do with how God manifests Himself in the midst of the fiery furnace. The revelation of Jesus can only come through circumstances. It is here and only here, where Jesus will appear – **"in the midst of a fiery furnace."**

For all those servants of the Lord who have been longing to know Jesus, get ready for the fiery furnace of affliction. God will allow all kinds of difficulty to come your way with the purpose of manifesting Jesus to you in a real way!

Many believers today are only "skin-deep." They only know of God's salvation and God's blessings. They have no clue what it means to walk in the "narrow" path with God. To most American believers, Christianity is nothing more than a religious club and nothing more.

People attend weekly meetings for the simple fact that that is what they should do on Sundays! They have not been broken by God's Holy Spirit, they have not been to the fiery furnace of affliction. The few have!

It's until we get in the furnace that Christ will appear and reveal Himself to us!

DEATH MUST PRECEDE BEFORE HIS GLORY APPEARS

"Now a certain man was sick, Lazarus of Bethany, the town of Mary and her sister Martha. It was that Mary who anointed the Lord with fragrant oil and wiped His feet with her hair, whose brother Lazarus was sick. Therefore, the sisters sent to Him, say-

ing, "Lord, behold, he whom You love is sick." When Jesus heard that, He said, "This sickness is not unto death, but for the glory of God, that the Son of God may be glorified through it." Now Jesus loved Martha and her sister and Lazarus. So, when He heard that he was sick, He stayed two more days in the place where He was. Then after this He said to the disciples, "Let us go to Judea again." (John 11:1-7)

"So when Jesus came, He found that he had already been in the tomb four days. Now Bethany was near Jerusalem, about two miles away. And many of the Jews had joined the women around Martha and Mary, to comfort them concerning their brother. Now Martha, as soon as she heard that Jesus was coming, went and met Him, but Mary was sitting in the house. Now Martha said to Jesus, "Lord, if You had been here, my brother would not have died. But even now I know that whatever You ask of God, God will give You." Jesus said to her, "Your brother will rise again." Martha said to Him," I know that he will rise again in the resurrection at the last day." Jesus said to her, "I am the resurrection and the life. He who believes in Me, though he may die, he shall live. And whoever lives and believes in Me shall never die. Do you believe this?" (John 11:17-26)

"Then Jesus, again groaning in Himself, came to the tomb. It was a cave, and a stone lay against it. Jesus said, "Take away the stone." Martha, the sister of him who was dead, said to Him, "Lord, by this time there is a stench, for he has been dead four days." Jesus said to her, "Did I not say to you that if you would believe you would see the glory of God?" Then they took away the stone from the place where the dead man was lying. And Jesus lifted up His eyes and said, "Father, I thank You that You have heard Me. And I know that You always hear Me, but because of the people who are standing by I said this, that they may believe that You sent Me." Now when He had said these things, He cried with a loud voice, "Lazarus, come forth!" (John 11:38-43)

Another method that God uses to reveal His glory is found in John 11. The Scripture teaches us that God loved Lazarus and his sisters. The Word reveals that Christ knew about the sickness of Lazarus and how it would eventually lead to his death.

Why was Christ not quick to get over to Lazarus house? Why when told about the sickness still waited two more days? Wasn't Lazarus a brother that Jesus loved?

Dear saints, please hear me. This is another of the Lord's ways in revealing His glory to His hungry servants, known as the few. God will allow the situation to be so "stinking dead," before He comes to take care of business. Jesus will allow the situation to be so out of human reach, before He comes to revive the dead.

In our own lives, Jesus will allow our dreams, plans and ideas to come to a grinding halt before He will reveal His heart and mind to us! God will not compete for your attention or mine. He will not get into a dual with other gods. He will not raise that which is still alive; He will patiently wait for death to do its perfect work, then He will come and resurrect us in a new and refined form.

If you have sincerely prayed for the Father to reveal Jesus to you in a greater way, then get ready for the fire of God to touch you. This is the way of the few. Remember, a fire goes before Him!

CHALLENGE YOURSELF and GO DEEPER WITH JESUS in CHAPTER 12

1. Have you found yourself becoming more and more hungry for Jesus?

2. If you haven't been growing more and more in your hunger for Jesus, have you asked the Lord why your spiritual appetite is missing from you?

3. Have you ever cried out to God and said, "Father, I want more of You!"

4. Have you ever experienced the fire of God in your own life?

5. Have you ever reached the point of total brokenness and helplessness? If you have, then know that you have found the secret to God's power. This is the way for "the few."

13

GOD'S HEART IS TO HAVE THE PREEMINENCE

If there is one thing that "the few" understand it is the fact that God must have the preeminence. They fully understand that no one is going to shine but Jesus, the King.

"He is the image of the invisible God, the firstborn over all creation. For by Him all things were created that are in heaven and that are on earth, visible and invisible, whether thrones or dominions or principalities or powers. All things were created through Him and for Him. And He is before all things, and in Him all things consist. And He is the head of the body, the church, who is the beginning, the firstborn from the dead, that in all things He may have the preeminence." (Colossians 1:15-18)

This powerful truth and principle has to do with Jesus Christ being first in everything we do. As born-again believers, Jesus has called us to a life of surrender and total dedication to Him. Our call as believers is one of intimacy with our Creator and total dependence upon Him.

It was God's idea to rescue sinners who by the way were helpless and couldn't do anything about it in way of redemption. It is this very fact that has qualified and made us partakers of this awesome salvation.

This story of redemption is one of a helpless people accepting the outstretched arms of a loving Savior. It is with this idea that I want to share this truth with you.

In the passage above we learn that Jesus made all things. The Scripture goes on to say that, "All things were created by Him and for Him." You and I were created by our Lord for Him. We are called to be partakers of His life and expressions of His nature here in this earth where He was rejected. When the Lord manifested His life in us, it was with the intent that we would abide there in that place of intimacy. Our life would be His life. Remember, "the few," are called to abide in Him and by doing this, they will produce much fruit for Him.

I am often asked from servants of the Lord, "What is God's will for my life?" The will of God can only be known in His habitation. As we abide in Him, the life of Christ Jesus will direct us unto our next move in Him.

Why are so many believers discouraged, lost and to a large degree confused? The answer: They are lacking intimacy and what it means to abide in Him.

Listen to the instruction of Jesus our Lord, **"Abide in Me, and I in you. As the branch cannot bear fruit of itself, unless it abides in the vine, neither can you, unless you abide in Me. "I am the vine, you are the branches. He who abides in Me, and I in him, bears much fruit; for without Me you can do nothing. If anyone does not abide in Me, he is cast out as a branch and is withered; and they gather them and throw them into the fire, and they are burned."** (John 15:4-7)

Jesus plainly allowed us to see that if we would abide in Him we would bear fruit. Again, He goes on to say, "If anyone does not abide in Me, he is cast out as a branch and is withered."

Let us look at some important facts here in this passage.

First, Jesus said, **"If anyone does not abide in Me, he is cast out as a branch and withered."** The word cast means ballo (bal'-lo); a primary verb; to throw (in various applications, more or less violent or intense).

I do not believe that the Lord is into 'yanking' people violently or intensely, but I do firmly believe that that is what it seems like when someone cuts themselves from abiding in God. They pull away from the life-giving flow of God.

The Scriptures also gives us the consequences of not abiding in Him. It says that we wither. The word wither also has meaning here; it means to dry up, to shrivel.

The reason for the drying up is because there is no longer life flowing through us. I don't believe that God yanks us from Him, but I do believe that it is very possible we can yank ourselves from the life-giving power when we neglect the abiding part of our walk with God.

To cut ourselves from this life-giving flow means automatic death or spiritual suicide, if you will.

I believe one of the most powerful weapons ever formed in hell is the sufficiency of man. The mindset that makes man think that he doesn't need his Creator to keep him living. This hellish plot from Satan wears many masks but in the end – it's all the same, man's ego and pride.

Our culture has made many believers think that simply by attending weekly church meetings, paying their tithes, and helping lend a hand here and there is sufficient to keep us close to God.

The only thing that will keep you and I close to the heart of God is our dependence upon God, our trust in God, and an ever-increasing intimate relationship with Jesus!

Man has said in his heart, "I don't need to be that spiritual – that is the preacher's job." Many have said, "Too much prayer and Bible reading can make you go crazy!" I don't know about making me go crazy, but surely, much prayer and Bible reading can only hold me accountable to my King!

THE REASON FOR "SMALL THINGS"

"After these things, Jesus went over the Sea of Galilee, which is the Sea of Tiberias. Then a great multitude followed Him, because they saw His signs which He performed on those who were diseased. And Jesus went up on the mountain, and there He sat with His disciples. Now the Passover, a feast of the Jews, was near. Then Jesus lifted up His eyes, and seeing a great multitude coming toward Him, He said to Philip, "Where shall we buy bread, that these may eat?" But this He said to test him, for He Himself knew what He would do. Philip answered Him, "Two hundred denarii worth of bread is not sufficient for them, that every one

GOD'S HEART IS TO HAVE THE PREEMINENCE

of them may have a little." One of His disciples, Andrew, Simon Peter's brother, said to Him, "There is a lad here who has five barley loaves and two small fish, but what are they among so many?" Then Jesus said, "Make the people sit down." Now there was much grass in the place. So the men sat down, in number about five thousand. And Jesus took the loaves, and when He had given thanks He distributed them to the disciples, and the disciples to those sitting down; and likewise of the fish, as much as they wanted." (John 6:1-11)

There is an interesting thing that takes place during the ministry of Jesus. He gets Himself in the middle of what would seem to be a "difficult" situation. Jesus knowing all things, **"for He Himself knew what He would do"** tested one of His followers – Phillip. He asked this future servant of God, **"Where shall we buy bread that these may eat?"** Remember, Jesus is here for a purpose: that in all things He may have the preeminence!

Jesus asked Phillip for an answer on how to feed this multitude of five thousand. Phillip, just like many of us believers today, he didn't recognize the power of God for a potential breakthrough in signs and wonders.

He turned to the arm of flesh and kept himself in a "conservative state" and answered logically and reasonably, **"Two hundred denarii worth of bread is not sufficient for them, that every one of them may have a little."**

It didn't matter that Phillip knew his math, it was going to take more than just adding up figures and coming up with some solution – it was going to take God to get this work done!

Jesus wants to have the preeminence in His body once again. He longs to be first; He longs to be magnified in the midst of the congregation once again! He is not looking for somebody to start counting his fingers and adding up numbers. He is looking for someone who can say, "I believe you are Jesus, the Son of the living God!" Nothing is too difficult for thee!"

Listen please, If the Lord has brought you to a situation in your life, no matter how difficult, no matter how impossible and no matter how adverse - if Jesus allowed that "thing" to be brought into your life, then you can be assured of something - He will also take you out, for "He Himself knew what He would do."

The reason you and I struggle on how we are going to "feed the multitudes" it's because we are so earthly-minded and God's miracle venue is in the heavens.

GOD'S HEART IS TO HAVE THE PREEMINENCE

It was Paul's burning desire for the believer to understand the power of seeking those things which are above.

"If then you were raised with Christ, seek those things which are above, where Christ is, sitting at the right hand of God. Set your mind on things above, not on things on the earth. For you died, and your life is hidden with Christ in God." (Colossians 3:1-3)

The carnal mind is enmity to God the Scripture says. It robs you and I of walking in the power of the supernatural. If Jesus is not having the preeminence in our lives every waking moment; if He is not first in our lives every waking moment, then we will succumb ourselves to the flesh and great will be the destruction thereof!

"But everyone who hears these sayings of Mine, and does not do them, will be like a foolish man who built his house on the sand: and the rain descended, the floods came, and the winds blew and beat on that house; and it fell. And great was its fall." (Matthew 7:26-27)

Giving the preeminence to Christ is not just listening to Him, but obeying His every command. It is here, where He is highly exalted. Our obedience gives Him the preeminence.

We will be tested time and time again, in the area of our personal faith. We would be wise to start listening to His voice and start to understand the ways of the Spirit. Jesus is altogether and totally one hundred and ten percent different than us.

When we come to the place where we truly understand that God has the preeminence, then we would have reached the mindset of "the few."

CHALLENGE YOURSELF and
GO DEEPER WITH JESUS in CHAPTER 13

1. The temptation of every believer is to get the glory that belongs to Christ. How have you managed to overcome this temptation in your own life?

2. The Lord wants to be our everything – do you find this fact an easy thing to practice in you daily life?

3. Jesus said, "Abide in Me." What does this mean to you in a personal way?

4. Have you been tested by the Lord in a way where He invited you to use whatever resources you presently had, even though it seemed that what you had at hand was not enough to meet the need?

5. I believe the Lord wants us to use whatever we have in hand. Would you like the Lord to use your life in a great way?

14

THE OTHER SIDE

"On the same day, when evening had come, He said to them, "Let us cross over to the other side." Now when they had left the multitude, they took Him along in the boat as He was. And other little boats were also with Him. And a great windstorm arose, and the waves beat into the boat, so that it was already filling. But He was in the stern, asleep on a pillow. And they awoke Him and said to Him, "Teacher, do You not care that we are perishing?" Then He arose and rebuked the wind, and said to the sea, "Peace, be still!" And the wind ceased and there was a great calm. But He said to them, "Why are you so fearful? How is it that you have no faith?" And they feared exceedingly, and said to one another, "Who can this be, that even the wind and the sea obey Him!" (Mark 4:35-41)

When one sets their heart to follow Jesus, he must prepare Himself for some of the greatest adventures in life. Following Jesus is everything but boring or stagnant. When we truly and wholeheartedly follow the Lord, our eyes will see and experience great things.

If you have been walking with Jesus for any short amount of time, you probably have experienced what it is to walk by faith. Walking by faith is simply believing what Jesus told you and keeping that course – till it is fulfilled. Now not everything just "falls into place" for many things will get in the way between "point A" and "point B." What are these things? If God has promised something to me, why do I have to fight to get to my destination?

Here is one principle that "the few" have adapted and have come to understand with greater insight.

I believe that God has full control of my life before, during, and after He gave me the promise. He is surely to complete that which He begins in me. My motivation to follow hard after Him should not be because of the reward that I will receive at the end. My motivation should be the awesome transformation into His likeness that takes place in me during my journey to the promise.

THE PROMISE IS GIVEN

In the text above, Jesus says to those who were following Him, "Let us cross over to the other side." It is obvious that Jesus had a desire to "go to the other side." Perhaps to continue to minister to others, either that or perhaps He was about to test the young followers in the school of faith. I believe the latter.

Many times, believers get all excited about some promise that God gave them. We should be excited about receiving a specific promise from the Lord, but too often the believer fails in receiving that promise due to unbelief.

God desires to unveil the secrets of His heart to anyone who would listen; He is willing to move through willing vessels as long as we are willing to believe Him! I have come to believe that Jesus is more interested in me learning and growing in "trusting faith" than the reward.

In the church today, believers in general, are so focused and consumed on the promise that they neglect totally what God has been longing to accomplish in them. I have spoken to believers who are bitter at someone or some church for not rewarding them accordingly. "It is not fair," they say. "I was mistreated and neglected." I have heard much "whining" about why they didn't receive the reward and how unfair things have been.

Oh Church, if we could get just a simple glimpse of the intents of God, even if it's for a second, we would be forever changed and on our way to a Christ-like transformation. "The few" get this.

Please remember, the promise is a picture of a destined future of something that God wants to accomplish through you but must work in you first. Therefore, the promise is God's means to unveil our very hearts before us. If we see things God's way, then we will understand that it is not about what I'm getting but what I'm learning to give as I walk on the way towards this promise.

THE WINDS AND THE WAVES

It is exciting to see someone get saved and give their hearts totally to Jesus. The bible says that heaven rejoices over a soul getting saved. I believe that with the same excitement and rejoicing, we should applaud one who is being tested in His walk with God and is overcoming and learning to lean on Christ for His victories.

The fulfillment of any promise is great, but the journey must be sweeter. If you can understand this, blessed are you.

The disciples were excited to be with Jesus and much more to follow Him wherever He went. As the invitation came to the disciples, they felt privileged as they were 'set apart' by Jesus to come with them to the other side.

How often we have felt so special simply because Jesus made some special promise or gave us a special calling to fulfill for Him? We rejoiced and even shared it with our friends of how God had shown us great favor only to find out that the "winds and waves" were just around the corner.

As the disciples made their short journey, Jesus falls asleep and the weather changes drastically. The Bible says that Jesus was asleep on a pillow while all this begins to take place. As the frantic disciples begin to see the winds blowing and water filling the boat, they begin to panic. After all, the sea is massive and it would be impossible to take the water out of the boat and many other thoughts begin to take consume their thinking.

They weren't thinking of the Word of the Lord which had been spoken earlier when Jesus said, "Let us cross over to the other side." All they were thinking was their own lives!

Any time that Jesus summons us to follow Him, it will quickly turn into a process of faith development. Something will have to die if we are to walk by faith. We cannot follow Jesus fully if we have some selfish agenda that is hidden in our hearts for God Himself will expose all flesh in the day of the **"winds and the waves."**

The testing is God's way of purifying our faith and makes it what it needs to be! I have learned by walking with the Lord that if we pray for God to use us or if we pray to see more of Jesus, it is inevitable that we will be confronted with the ugliness of our hearts. God's **"winds and waves"** will come into our boat and force us to call on the name of the Lord.

The children of Israel had many promises given to them as they journeyed from Egypt through the wilderness and into the promise land. It all seemed to be flowing their way until they got thirsty and hungry. When the flesh begins to cry out, the test has begun. Were they willing to pay the price of leaning on Jehovah for all their provision? Would they get restless and begin to accuse Moses, God's servant of what they were experiencing? Apparently, Israel failed the test miserably and got mad at God. Listen to their fearful hearts:

"And the people thirsted there for water, and the people complained against Moses, and said, "Why is it you have brought us up out of Egypt, to kill us and our children and our livestock with thirst?" (Exodus 17:3)

The resounding question was, **"Why is it you have brought us up out of Egypt, to kiss us and our children and our livestock with thirst?"** The reason God brought them out is so they could be free to worship and serve God and now as they are being tested, they are saying God is trying to kill them.

The disciples of Jesus were in essence saying the same thing: **"And they awoke Him and said to Him, "Teacher, do You not care that we are perishing?"** The disciples of Jesus were fearful for their lives and didn't understand why they were going through all that they were experiencing. When Jesus said to them let us cross to the other side, they got excited. When the test came, their unbelief was exposed!

It was the same way with Israel of old: they wanted to follow God out of the land of Egypt for the purpose of attaining a promise, but when the test came they truly didn't believe God and the promise given to them.

Any time that our hearts have been touched by God to walk in a higher dimension, our faith and our perseverance will be tested. Every promise of God is preceded with great testing. When you tell Jesus, "I will follow You Lord," He will test Your resolve, your commitment to Him.

HINDRANCE TO THE PROMISE

"For who, having heard, rebelled? Indeed, was it not all who came out of Egypt, led by Moses? Now with whom was He angry forty years? Was it not with those who sinned, whose corpses fell in the wilderness? And to whom did He swear that they would not enter

His rest, but to those who did not obey? So we see that they could not enter in because of unbelief." (Hebrews 3:16-19)

The Bible clearly states that it was unbelief that kept the children of Israel from coming into the Promise Land. It will be unbelief that will keep us from God's best for us. It will be unbelief that will keep us in such stagnation.

Unless we are willing to humble ourselves before God and allow Him to speak to us the prophetic word, we will never experience God's dimension in a greater way.

One of the reasons that many servants of the Lord are moving with God and accomplishing His will here on earth is because of this truth – they simply have seen the Lord and believe in what He is saying to them. They are moving according to God's timetable, God's drumbeat and in God's anointing.

JESUS INSTRUCTS

Before I close this truth, I want you to look at the last part of Mark 4.

After Jesus had quieted the storm, He turns to the disciples and says, "Why are you so fearful? How is it that you have no faith?" And they feared exceedingly, and said to one another, **"Who can this be, that even the wind and the sea obey Him!"** Those were some sharp words coming from Jesus. It almost seems that Jesus was trying to get them to understand that faith in Him was going to be the only way to victory in any sphere.

He points out two things: fear and no faith. Fear is a fruit of the flesh and faith is the enemy of fear.

When these two things are present in us, we will be spiritually paralyzed.

When fear and no faith are predominant in our lives it is almost as if we are in a straight-jacket, unable to move or do anything.

How do we get out of this? The disciples gave us the answer in the following sentence, **"Who can this be, that even the wind and the sea obey Him!"**

Their fear and lack of faith came because they didn't know Him. They didn't know His ways, His heart, His mind and methods. They had been with Him, but they didn't know Him. There are many in church today who don't know Him, thus their carnal lifestyle and rebellious ways.

CHALLENGE YOURSELF and GO DEEPER WITH JESUS in CHAPTER 14

1. The Lord is constantly challenging us to walk with Him to unknown places. Where was the last place God invited you to walk with Him?

2. Every promise has a condition to it, be ready to follow through when God gives you a personal promise.

3. Every invitation requires a certain level of faith. Only through faith, one can see the path to the promise.

4. With every step of faith that you take, you will go deeper. It might get scary, but don't fear! God will take you through, if you hold on to the promise.

15

"I CAN'T WAIT TO FALL IN LOVE WITH JESUS AGAIN!"

The fact that one walks close to Jesus or hand in hand with Jesus, doesn't mean that you won't have off times where you can go a bit cold or indifferent with God. The few, this company of God's disciples, know all too well about the danger of losing their touch of God. It can happen to anyone for that matter. Read on.

WHERE DID THE LOVE FOR JESUS GO?

I would like to begin by saying that many believers today find themselves in a spiritually "cold" stage in their walk with Jesus and wonder where they went wrong. There are some who feel that due to many tests and trials the life has been "taken out" of them, yet there are others who are puzzled by the ugly compromise that rises from within them. "How could I have done such a thing," they say, "that is not me!"

How does all this coldness creep in into our hearts? Where did we go wrong? Where did my commitment and allegiance to Jesus go? I am speaking of a subject that very few Christians would care to admit, but it's true!

Many believers have lost their anointing and are now cold and indifferent in the things of the Lord. Why? Let us look at some valuable guidance in the Word of God.

"To the angel of the church of Ephesus write, 'These things says He who holds the seven stars in His right hand, who walks in the midst of the seven golden lampstands: "I know your works, your labor, your patience, and that you cannot bear those who are evil. And you have tested those who say they are apostles and are not, and have found them liars; and you have persevered and have patience, and have labored for My name's sake and have not become weary. Nevertheless I have this against you, that you have left your first love. Remember therefore from where you have fallen; repent and do the first works, or else I will come to you quickly and remove your lampstand from its place – unless you repent." (Revelation 2:1-5)

In these verses, the Holy Spirit through the hands of John the Beloved, brings forth a strong and to some degree "hidden" problem in the church of Ephesus. The Lord Jesus quickly recognizes the Ephesian church as a church that was great in the "works" department. Of them, Jesus said, **"I know your works..."**

It is obvious that this church was a hard-working church. Here's my question: If it was such a hard-working church, why did Jesus wrote them such a stern warning or message?

HIDING BEHIND GREAT WORKS FOR GOD

Let me now cover this "hidden" problem in the church of Ephesus. The Scripture says that Jesus commended them and said, **"I know your works, your labor, your patience, and that you cannot bear those who are evil. And you have tested those who say they are apostles and are not, and have found them liars; and you have persevered and have patience, and have labored for My name's sake and have not become weary."**

Jesus was applauding this church's great works. He was excited about their "outward" manifestations of loyalty to the work of God. Was this the kind of works that would make our Lord truly content? Were outward works what He was really looking for?

In our "American" gospel mentality, many believers think that outward works is truly what God is looking for. Many pastors have fallen into the same trap. They feel that simply because there is much activity going on in their churches and ministries, God is very pleased.

"I CAN'T WAIT TO FALL IN LOVE WITH JESUS AGAIN!"

The Ephesian church seemed to be doing good as far as "attempting great things for Jesus," but in the process of "attempting," they were backsliding.

Many believers, including ministers, hide behind this curtain of "great works." They convince themselves by saying, "Look all that God is doing" and pay little attention to what is really required by the Lord. "The few" are those who are watchful regarding this.

I am reminded of a common-day alcoholic. He has some major issues in his heart, but won't deal with the issue. Instead he takes another drink. Drink upon drink, but all along falling into greater stupor. Many believers fall into this same state (but to some degree worse). They say, "I'm ok" but "they are dying spiritually."

WHAT REALLY MATTERS TO GOD

I believe God praises the hard worker; I believe God honors him or her whose desire is to carry out good things for the sake of kingdom advancement. But I also believe that these things, as good and great as they may be, they don't substitute for an intimate walk with Jesus. You can pay your tithes, you can come to church every single time the doors open, but if you are not in love with Jesus – You don't know Him. God is once again calling out to "the few!"

"Not everyone who says to Me, 'Lord, Lord,' shall enter the kingdom of heaven, but he who does the will of My Father in heaven. Many will say to Me in that day, 'Lord, Lord, have we not prophesied in Your name, cast out demons in Your name, and done many wonders in Your name?' And then I will declare to them, 'I never knew you; depart from Me, you who practice lawlessness!' (Matthew 7:21-23)

The Ephesian Church had come to a place where they were more focused on the work of God than the God of the work.

When we begin to focus on anything other than Jesus – our spiritual lives will begin to shake! We will lose our discernment first. When discernment leaves us, all we have is our soulish [carnal] nature to go by. Is it any wonder that much of the work of God is done in the flesh? Is it any wonder that much depression over takes us and even governs our lives?

I am a firm believer in that Christians must develop and intimate walk with Jesus if they are to overcome their selfish nature, this wicked world and a mad devil.

What matters to God is that we know His Son – Jesus Christ in an intimate way. What matters to God is that we get close to His heart and learn to sit at His feet and learn instruction for our everyday situations. Can you hear me church? Or are you still lacking understanding?

HOW AND WHERE DID WE LOSE THAT LOVE FOR JESUS?

Before I expound to you what I believe has been the cause for losing our love for Jesus, I would like for you to ask yourself the question: Do I truly love Jesus more today than I've ever loved Him? If your answer is yes – then keep going! If your answer is no, not sure, or a little - than keep your spiritual ears open.

THE BELOVED (Jesus Christ)
      Like a lily among thorns, so is my love among the daughters.

THE SHULAMITE (the church or the disciple)

Like an apple tree among the trees of the woods, so is my beloved among the sons. I sat down in his shade with great delight, and his fruit was sweet to my taste.

THE SHULAMITE TO THE DAUGHTERS OF JERUSALEM
(the church, the disciple, testify…)

"He brought me to the banqueting house, and his banner over me was love. Sustain me with cakes of raisins, refresh me with apples, for I am lovesick. His left hand is under my head, and his right hand embraces me. I charge you, O daughters of Jerusalem, by the gazelles or by the does of the field." (Song of Solomon 2:2-7)

By reading these first seven verses, we discover that Jesus and His church have an awesome thing going. They are very much in love. Up to this point, the believer can only talk about the awesomeness of her Beloved! The Scripture goes on to note that the Shulamite (disciple) said, "I am lovesick." The word lovesick here means to be so overwhelmed by love that it makes one weak.

The relationship with our Lord should continually be at this stage. We should always cultivate this type of love in our spirit.

THE TESTS AND TRIALS OF CHARACTER BUILDING

Sometimes our love for Jesus is tested severely by situations that are beyond our control. We are brought to a place of desperation and are called to walk by faith not by sight.

As we venture to "make-ends" meet, solitude, loneliness and incredible feelings of abandonment surround us. Where praises used to sound off in the name of Jesus are no longer heard!

Where worship was an attitude of heart; it has now become nothing but echoes of meaningless words! Have you ever been at this place? These trials were so hard that you don't know if you can be as near to Jesus as you once were!

THE SHULAMITE

"The voice of my beloved! Behold, he comes Leaping upon the mountains, skipping upon the hills. My beloved is like a gazelle or a young stag. Behold, he stands behind our wall; He is looking through the windows, Gazing through the lattice. My beloved spoke, and said to me: "Rise up, my love, my fair one, and come away. For lo, the winter is past, the rain is over and gone. The flowers appear on the earth; the time of singing has come, and the voice of the turtledove is heard in our land. The fig tree puts forth her green figs, and the vines with the tender grapes give a good smell. Rise up, my love, my fair one, and come away!" (Song of Solomon 2:7-13)

After the trial is over, the Lord bits us to come away and be with Him. He wants to embrace us once again and put His hand under our heads. He has come to take us away into His banqueting house.

If we neglect His voice when He calls us to "come away," we will miss His time for intimacy with us. We will totally miss out on God's touch upon us. We must be quick to hear and obey Him at any cost.

ARISING AFTER THE HEART OF GOD

THE SHULAMITE

"By night on my bed I sought the one I love; I sought him, but I did not find him. "I will rise now," I said, "And go about the city; in the streets and in the squares I will seek the one I love." I sought him, but I did not find him. The watchmen who go about the city found me; I said, "Have you seen the one I love?" Scarcely had I passed by them, when I found the one I love. I held him and would not let him go, until I had brought him to the house of my mother, and into the chamber of her who conceived me." (Song of Solomon 3:1-4)

The love of God is cultivated by our attentiveness in hearing His call to intimacy. It is not the other way around - where we come when were good and ready. God will beckon our hearts to come and meet Him: we either obey or disobey.

We could learn something on this matter by listening to David's

Psalm: "When You said, **"Seek My face, "My heart said to You, "Your face, LORD, I will seek."** (Psalm 27:8)

Church, the first love which Jesus talked about is in relation to an intimate love for God. Works are good, but intimacy [first love] will not be burned in the fire of God's judgment on that day! [**. . . each one's work will become clear; for the Day will declare it, because it will be revealed by fire; and the fire will test each one's work, of what sort it is. If anyone's work which he has built on it endures, he will receive a reward. If anyone's work is burned, he will suffer loss; but he himself will be saved, yet so as through fire."**] (1 Corinthians 3:13-15)

Let us press into God's heart through Jesus our Lord. Repent if you need to repent; come clean with the Lord, get washed in His blood. Acknowledge your need for intimacy with Him and He will meet you. Amen.

"I CAN'T WAIT TO FALL IN LOVE WITH JESUS AGAIN!"

CHALLENGE YOURSELF and
GO DEEPER WITH JESUS in CHAPTER 15

1. Do you ever feel "cold in the Lord?"

2. Good works are great; only thing is that they are not a substitute for an intimate relationship with Jesus and the Father.

3. Make sure that you are not just doing good works for the sake of good works. Make sure that Jesus is leading you into them.

4. The Lord will call you to "come away" with Him many times; make sure to listen and be quick to obey this one important call.

16

OBEDIENCE GOES BEFORE THE BLESSING

"Then the word of the LORD came to him, saying, "Arise, go to Zarephath, which belongs to Sidon, and dwell there. See, I have commanded a widow there to provide for you." So he arose and went to Zarephath. And when he came to the gate of the city, indeed a widow was there gathering sticks. And he called to her and said, "Please bring me a little water in a cup, that I may drink." And as she was going to get it, he called to her and said, "Please bring me a morsel of bread in your hand." So she said, "As the LORD your God lives, I do not have bread, only a handful of flour in a bin, and a little oil in a jar; and see, I am gathering a couple of sticks that I may go in and prepare it for myself and my son, that we may eat it, and die." And Elijah said to her, "Do not fear; go and do as you have said, but make me a small cake from it first, and bring it to me; and afterward make some for yourself and your son. For thus says the LORD God of Israel: 'The bin of flour shall not be used up, nor shall the jar of oil run dry, until the day the LORD sends rain on the earth.'" So she went away and did according to the word of Elijah; and she and he and her household ate for many days. The bin of flour was not used up, nor did the jar of oil run dry, according to the word of the LORD which He spoke by Elijah." (1 Kings 17:8-16)

Let me bring you into something I believe to be a great truth, which the few walk out. This truth will put us on a course that will reveal to us what it means to follow Jesus in a deeper way – a way that makes us totally dependent upon His provision and His daily care.

Many disciples are not at this spiritual place in their walk with Him, but will quickly learn that unless God is the One providing, every well of provision, and I mean every well of provision in this world will run dry.

Please note that it is so like God to bring us to a place where we learn to walk by faith. Faith is the only way in God to understand Him in a fuller way.

The Lord will gently bring us to a place where we will have to make a choice; we either stay in Him or we take it upon ourselves to make ends meet.

These Scriptures will quicken our minds and the Holy Ghost will turn His light upon us to see this awesome subject.

THE WIDOW AT ZAREPHATH

As we come to the story before us, we discover that the Prophet Elijah had been sent by God to Zarephath, which stood for the (place of dyeing) - a Phoenician coastal city situated between Tyre and Sidon; it was north of Jerusalem) where he would come across a poor widow who would eventually provide for Him. It is interesting to notice that God would use the poor to feed the poor. Now, Elijah was rich in God – and the widow was about to learn how to be rich in God.

God was about to unleash the most powerful lesson given to mankind on how to be rich in God. Jesus spoke of this when He taught His disciples on giving:

"Then He spoke a parable to them, saying: "The ground of a certain rich man yielded plentifully. And he thought within himself, saying, 'What shall I do, since I have no room to store my crops?' So he said, 'I will do this: I will pull down my barns and build greater, and there I will store all my crops and my goods. And I will say to my soul, "Soul, you have many goods laid up for many years; take your ease; eat, drink, and be merry."' But God said to him, 'Fool! This night your soul will be required of you; then whose will those things be which you have provided?' "So is he who lays up treasure for himself, and is not rich toward God." (Luke 12:16-21)

We must learn to recognize God in our giving. Anytime that the Lord draws near to you, it is always an opportunity for us to give ourselves fully to Him. This is the law in God's economy.

WHY A WIDOW, OH GOD?!

I would like to turn your attention away from Elijah and focus ourselves on the poor widow from Zarephath.

By reading the Scriptures, we find that the widow was in a very tight spot, for the famine had finally taken its toll and her son and her were about to die shortly.

As the woman is contemplating her fate, a prophet shows up at her house and asks for water. She had no problem giving him a cup of water. Remember, it is God testing the widow, we as believers, represent that widow.

To give the prophet a cup of water presented no challenge for her. She quickly went to get him a cup. The challenge and lesson of faith came when Elijah called her and said: "And as she was going to get it, he called to her and said, **"Please bring me a morsel of bread in your hand."** (1 Kings 17:11) God knew that this woman was clinging to something that was precious to her. She was clinging to her only hope of life – one last meal!

Dear servant, how many times have we held on to something that we felt was our only hope for living? Though the Lord asked us for it, we refuse to let it go. Though the Lord wanted to reveal Himself strong on our behalf, we never saw His power – for we wouldn't let the "one thing" go!

"So she said, "As the LORD your God lives, I do not have bread, only a handful of flour in a bin, and a little oil in a jar; and see, I am gathering a couple of sticks that I may go in and prepare it for myself and my son, that we may eat it, and die." (1 Kings 17:12)

When God comes in and turns His search light on in our hearts - instead of humbling ourselves before Him, we start making excuses for not releasing the "one thing." And boy, are we creative when it comes to letting go!

BLESSINGS WITHOUT CONDITIONS, NOT GOD'S WAY

In the church world today, especially in our western culture, we have taught believers the opposite. We have taught people that all they need to do is come and get prayed for and everything will be fine after that.

We must remember something: Nothing happens without the hand of God moving it! If we find ourselves in a "tight spot," remember, God brought us here. The question we must not fail to ask is: "Lord, why have you brought me here?

If there is rebellion in my heart, God will deal with that first. Why should I be asking God to bless me where there is willful disobedience reigning in my heart? Does this make sense to you? I must get in line with God's will and then trust Him for His supply.

JESUS KNOWS OUR HEARTS

When the Lord appears to us by way of revelation, He will deal first with self. He will be quick to point out those things that are robbing Him of His glory; He will bring forth to those things which are hindering the flow of His blessing.

Remember that Jesus will strip us from everything that hinders His Lordship in our lives. He wants to be everything to us all the time!

The widow was holding on to something that God had need of that very hour – bread for His servant. God was looking for obedience in that widow's heart...it is when we are the nearest to God that we can understand this sacrificial lifestyle. Apparently, it doesn't make any sense that God would use a poor and needy widow to carry out His purposes, being that she was void of substance.

I'm sure there were many rich people in the times of Elijah which God could have used to feed this servant. Instead, He chose a poor and needy widow! It doesn't make sense to the carnal mind! Then again God's most powerful vessels are the broken ones.

Jesus said, **"Blessed are the poor in spirit, for theirs is the kingdom of heaven."** (Matthew 5:3) The word poor means beggar. These whom Jesus is referring to are a people who are continually in their spirit begging for more of Jesus. These understand heaven and the things that pertain to eternity.

CONTINUAL OBEDIENCE IS KEY TO GOD'S PROVISION

"And Elijah said to her, "Do not fear; go and do as you have said, but make me a small cake from it first, and bring it to me; and afterward make some for yourself and your son. For thus says the LORD God of Israel: 'The bin of flour shall not be used up, nor shall the jar of oil run dry, until the day the LORD sends rain on the earth.'" So she went away and did according to the word of Elijah; and she and he and her household ate for many days. The bin of flour was not used up, nor did the jar of oil run dry, accord-

ing to the word of the LORD which He spoke by Elijah." (1 Kings 17:13-16)

In the case of this widow, God, through Elijah the prophet was daring her to trust the Word of the Lord. The key word I want to bring forth is the word first. Elijah told her, **"Do not fear; go and do as you have said, but make me a small cake from it first, and bring it to me; and afterward make some for yourself and your son."** The word first here means first, in place, time, or rank.

In other words, the prophet was saying, "Put God first and then you. Let God arise within you and don't let the flesh lead you!"

The prophet Elijah told the widow that if she would step-out and obey His words, that **'The bin of flour shall not be used up, nor shall the jar of oil run dry…'** Does this mean that it would never run dry? No!

It meant that so long as God was involved and she was doing what God wanted her to do – it would never go dry!

It is the same way when God calls us to walk with Him. He promises to keep us supplied with everything needed to carry out His holy purposes on the earth!

When we are walking in obedience we are removed from all responsibility to make anything happen. We don't have to keep nothing floating – He will!

When He calls us out to do impossible feats this means that along with that call to obedience – God's provision is not far.

CHALLENGE YOURSELF and
GO DEEPER WITH JESUS in CHAPTER 16

1. Do you feel God challenging you lately to a deeper walk of faith and commitment?

2. God will always ask for that "one thing" that you love the most. Are you ready to give it all up and trust Him with the outcome?

3. God does know all our needs, but He needs an excuse to bless you. He might ask you to feed the hungry before He releases resources to your life. Keep your eyes open for this.

4. As long as we obey - we will never run dry. All dryness is a sign of God not being present there. Ask yourself why.

17

RECOGNIZING DOORS OF OPPORTUNITY

"Elisha had become sick with the illness of which he would die. Then Joash the king of Israel came down to him, and wept over his face, and said, "O my father, my father, the chariots of Israel and their horsemen!" And Elisha said to him, "Take a bow and some arrows. "So he took himself a bow and some arrows. Then he said to the king of Israel, "Put your hand on the bow." So he put his hand on it, and Elisha put his hands on the king's hands. And he said, "Open the east window"; and he opened it. Then Elisha said, "Shoot"; and he shot. And he said, "The arrow of the LORD's deliverance and the arrow of deliverance from Syria; for you must strike the Syrians at Aphek till you have destroyed them." Then he said, "Take the arrows "; so he took them. And he said to the king of Israel, "Strike the ground"; so he struck three times, and stopped. And the man of God was angry with him, and said, "You should have struck five or six times; then you would have struck Syria till you had destroyed it! But now you will strike Syria only three times." (2 Kings 13:14-19)

The message that the Lord would have us see relates to God making or opening awesome opportunities for our lives.

I want to address that God does open doors for us and if we are courageous we will see the fruit of our obedience!

The few have come to know this one truth. They don't look at other people to see what they are doing; no, they look to God for prophetic direction in their lives.

Much of the whining and complaining you hear in the mouth of believers today has nothing to with unfairness or injustice. I dare say that most of the complaining going around, relates to "passed-up" opportunities in their lives. In other words, God opened a door of opportunity but we didn't like it, so we disobeyed! We are now reaping the fruit of our disobedience.

In the story mentioned above, God was about to do an awesome work. He had come to the aid of King Joash by using His servant Elisha. The armies were "ganging up" on King Joash and he cried out to the man of God. Elisha then gave the king some specific instructions to follow which he did to a certain point. It is this that I want to bring to attention to – half-hearted obedience!

"STRIKE THE GROUND"

Elisha the prophet specifically told the King to take the arrows and to strike the ground with them. Was this a hard thing to do? Probably not! The King did as Elisha commanded him, but he only struck the arrow three times. He only did what was in his own heart but did not do what was in the heart of God! Is this a serious matter? You bet!

If you notice something here, the prophet never told him how many times to strike the arrows on the ground – he basically told him to "strike the ground." When God commands us to do something, we don't stop till He tells us. This should be an everlasting principle to those who truly follow Christ, the few.

Often the Lord commands us to carry out something in His Name and we go so far and then we turn back. We go the whole ninety percent but no further. We go right to the end of the test and before God can deliver us – we give up! We go the point of being broken and when it really starts to crack, we quickly reach for more clay and patch it up!

Jesus faced the same ordeal when He spent that night at Gethsemane. This was high time. God had been speaking to Him regarding His future and what was to come upon Him. No one knew the mind of God but Christ at that holy moment.

As the night proceeded and as the disciples "dreamed on," the soldiers came to where Jesus was seeking for Him. **"When Jesus had spoken these words, He went out with His disciples over the Brook Kidron, where there was a garden, which He and His disciples entered. And Judas, who betrayed Him, also knew the place; for Jesus often met there with His disciples. Then Judas, having received a detachment of troops, and officers from the chief priests and Pharisees, came there with lanterns, torches, and weapons. Jesus therefore, knowing all things that would come upon Him, went forward and said to them, "Whom are you seeking?" They answered Him, "Jesus of Nazareth." Jesus said to them, "I am He." And Judas, who betrayed Him, also stood with them. Now when He said to them, "I am He," they drew back and fell to the ground. Then He asked them again, "Whom are you seeking?" And they said, "Jesus of Nazareth." Jesus answered, "I have told you that I am He. Therefore, if you seek Me, let these go their way,"** that the saying might be fulfilled which He spoke, **"Of those whom You gave Me I have lost none." Then Simon Peter, having a sword, drew it and struck the high priest's servant, and cut off his right ear. The servant's name was Malchus. So Jesus said to Peter, "Put your sword into the sheath. Shall I not drink the cup which My Father has given Me?"** (John 18:1-11)

If you will notice here that Jesus was not "patching-up" the crack on the pot, He was a willing vessel waiting to be broken for His Father sake. He didn't stop moving forward with God's plan just because He wanted to. He was under marching orders and that is what King Joash was under. He was to continue beating the ground with those arrows until Elisha would tell him to stop. Are you getting this?

WHY WAS ELISHA ANGRY?

"And he said to the king of Israel, "Strike the ground"; so he struck three times, and stopped. And the man of God was angry with him, and said, "You should have struck five or six times; then you would have struck Syria till you had destroyed it! But now you will strike Syria only three times."

I believe that nothing disappoints the heart of God more than disobedience on our part. This king's future would have been established if only He would have kept on going till he was told to stop – Syria would have been destroyed! But now they would only strike them three times but eventually Syria would recover.

Striking the arrows on the ground three times may not be a big deal to us, but what Elisha saw was the passivity with which this king struck the ground. This act revealed King Joash's heart! He wasn't willing to go further than what his carnal mind thought he should have. In essence, King Joash said, "I will do this three times and if God wants to do the rest ...so be it!"

There are many believers who don't recognize the opportunities that God makes for them. God opens the door for you to be a blessing to someone else and you only do the minimum. Only what is expected from you – you do!

There is no real desire to be a blessing. These people are nothing but takers and one day they will learn that with the same measure they used on someone else; this will be the same measure that God will use on them. Can you see it!

I think God wants to bring His people to a place where we break free from this "careful" spirit. It's alright to want to be careful with things, but it's altogether different when we are careful to a fault – even when it comes to blessing a people with a special love offering or alms.

I have discovered that when the Lord tells me to do something for Him, as I move in obedience to His heart, God has blessed me greatly. Whether it has been an issue of giving money, giving time or even when it came to spend some time in intercession for someone.

We must learn not to stop just because we feel we have already done our part. We must persevere until the burden that God has laid upon our hearts ceases and until we know that we know, that we have attained that which the Holy Spirit has cried out for us.

I believe that more than God being angry, disappointment is what floods His heart. Eventually the Lord will get angry and will have to discipline our actions of apathy and selfishness.

FROM SPIRIT TO FLESH

"Are you so foolish? Having begun in the Spirit, are you now being made perfect by the flesh?" (Galatians 3:3)

This matter of being obedient to God when He tells us to move forward with Him is a crucial one – for our future and destiny are involved. King Joash started being obedient, but then lost heart somewhere in the battle.

The Galatian brothers had started to follow the true gospel – the gospel that came by the Spirit by faith. They were so convinced this was God's way, but then false teachers got a hold of them. They started teaching them that they need to keep the Law [flesh]. Paul comes back to them and says, "How could you be so foolish [which means intellect; the mind or human mind and feeling; sensual].

What Paul is really saying is, "How could you let human reasoning overthrow the Holy Spirit's direction for your life?"

Dear servants of Jesus, we need God to help us stay in focus when it comes to obedience! Let us not begin to reason in our minds that which is of God and end up with a "fleshly" decision. This could truly disable our future destiny.

GOING THE EXTRA MILE – ATTITUDE OF THE HEART

"You have heard that it was said, 'An eye for an eye and a tooth for a tooth.' But I tell you not to resist an evil person. But whoever slaps you on your right cheek, turn the other to him also. If anyone wants to sue you and take away your tunic, let him have your cloak also. And whoever compels you to go one mile, go with him two. Give to him who asks you, and from him who wants to borrow from you do not turn away." (Matthew 5:38-42)

The safest way to enter God's promises, is if we develop "the extra mile" attitude. This principle has to do when we say to ourselves, "I will obey God until He changes or stops me from doing the last command He gave me. In the meantime, I will go the extra mile!"

When the door of opportunity opens, keep this principle in mind. If a door is opened before you it's not because you opened it – God did. So, what should be our response as to this open door? We walk through it until God says stop.

CHALLENGE YOURSELF and
GO DEEPER WITH JESUS in CHAPTER 17

1. Have you ever felt like you had passed on God-given opportunities?

2. When you hear the words "half-hearted obedience" – what comes to your mind?

3. Have you ever done 99% of God's will and avoided the 1% percent. How did you know that you didn't go all the way? (meditate on this)

4. Remember: Do more than what you were asked to do or planned to do. This is one of the keys to get a promotion in God!

5. Are you practicing "the extra mile" standard and attitude in your life?

18

RENEWING OUR LIVES IN THE HOLY GHOST

"And do not be drunk with wine, in which is dissipation; but be filled with the Spirit..." (Ephesians 5:18)

Paul's admonition to the church at Ephesus was for them to not be drunk with wine but to be filled with more of Jesus - to be filled with the Spirit. The word filled in the Greek means to make replete, i.e. (literally) to cram (a net), level up (a hollow).

It was Paul's burning passion that every believer would be filled 'to the brim' with the Holy Ghost. It was a cry that God put in his heart for the church of Jesus Christ. It was a strong conviction in the Apostle's heart that anyone who called on the name of the Lord would be filled with more of Jesus. It is the same with those who belong to "the few."

There is much talk about the Holy Spirit in our Pentecostal and charismatic circles. Many people go around saying that they have been filled and are now operating in all the gifts of the Spirit. Many think that simply because they speak in tongues they have been exempt from walking uprightly before God.

I heard a story once about a so-called man of God who claimed that God ministered though him powerfully. He was in Las Vegas, Nevada ministering to a church in the evening service when He greeted the people by saying that he had been down at the bar drinking some cocktails and as he was about to take his third cocktail, the Holy Ghost came to him and told him, "Two cocktails is enough, you don't need the third one!" To this I say, 'Will the real Holy Spirit please stand up!'

The very name of the Holy Spirit tells us what the third person of the trinity is all about. He is the Holy Spirit, not the Un-Holy Spirit. The word Holy means to be separated unto God! To be holy means that you and I are God's property! We are not even our own, we were bought with a price.

"Or do you not know that your body is the temple of the Holy Spirit who is in you, whom you have from God, and you are not your own? For you were bought at a price; therefore glorify God in your body and in your spirit, which are God's." (1 Corinthians 6:19-20)

OUR LIVES KEPT AND EMPOWERED BY THE SPIRIT

When you and I came to Jesus, we were born from above – born from God to be kept by God and empowered by God. His Spirit was given to us as the agent that would bring us to Christ and teach us Christ and express Christ. The Holy Spirit was given to us to show us the ways of God – His holy ways!

The Scripture says,
"However, when He, the Spirit of truth, has come, He will guide you into all truth ; for He will not speak on His own authority, but whatever He hears He will speak; and He will tell you things to come. He will glorify Me, for He will take of what is Mine and declare it to you." (John 16:13-14)

In this portion of Scripture, Jesus told His disciples that the Holy Spirit would teach them all truth. It was this same Holy Spirit that was to live in them and teach them twenty-four hours a day seven days a week.

You might wonder why the "big spill" regarding the renewal in the Holy Spirit. Let me just say that if you don't renew yourself in the Holy Spirit, you will suffer greatly or should I say gravely?

Jesus said that the Holy Spirit would "guide" the disciples. The word guide means to show the way; a teacher. I need to be renewed in the Holy Spirit simply because I need to be shown the way!

The Holy Spirit will keep me close to the heart of Jesus. He will not only guide me but also will reveal to me the deep things of God. **"But as it is written: "Eye has not seen, nor ear heard, nor have entered into the heart of man the things which God has prepared for those who love Him." But God has revealed them to us through His Spirit. For the Spirit searches all things, yes, the deep things of God."** (1 Corinthians 2:9-10)

What are the deep things of God? The word deep in this verse means mystery. The Holy Spirit will reveal to us the "mysteries" of God.

Another thing that happens in us when we are renewed in the Holy Spirit is that of power. **"But you shall receive power when the Holy Spirit has come upon you; and you shall be witnesses to Me in Jerusalem, and in all Judea and Samaria, and to the end of the earth."** (Acts 1:8)

The Holy Spirit will give us power to be a witness for Jesus. He will give us power to declare the full counsel of God to all who would hear.

The reason many people are not touched by God when they first meet us is because there is no manifestation of the presence of God in our lives. There is simply no power! We are no different than the people we talk to: they don't have any power and we don't have any power...what is the difference?

The Holy Ghost comes into our lives and renews us with the same passion Jesus had for the lost. He will make us groan, weep and sacrifice for the lost! The Holy Spirit will simply continue to carry out through us the wishes of Jesus.

THE NEED FOR HOLY FIRE

"But when he saw many of the Pharisees and Sadducees coming to his baptism, he said to them, "Brood of vipers! Who warned you to flee from the wrath to come? Therefore bear fruits worthy of repentance, and do not think to say to yourselves, 'We have Abraham as our father.' For I say to you that God is able to raise up children to Abraham from these stones. And even now the ax is laid to the root of the trees. Therefore every tree which does not bear good fruit is cut down and thrown into the fire. I indeed baptize you with water unto repentance, but He who is coming after me is mightier than I, whose sandals I am not worthy to carry. He will baptize you with the Holy Spirit and fire. His winnowing fan is in His hand, and He will thoroughly clean out His threshing floor, and gather His wheat into the barn; but He will burn up the chaff with unquenchable fire." (Matthew 3:7-12)

One other thing that the Holy Spirit will renew in us when we come to Him in total humility and in need is the fire of His holiness. He will bring us to Himself and impart a burning desire that says, 'I want to be so close to God!'

The Pharisees and Sadducees wanted to be partakers of this baptism John was promoting at the Jordan River. When they got there, John laid out the law, the way it was!

What John is really saying, "You can say that you are Abraham's father and that you have descendants that walked with God, but you don't walk with God. This baptism is a symbol for all to see that you follow God, but it is really God that will release the fire in your hearts to make you perfect for Him!" John went on to say, **"He will baptize you with the Holy Spirit and fire."** To receive or to be renewed in the Holy Spirit means that fire has come to your heart to do away with all that is not of God.

WHY ALL THE WHINING IN THE KINGDOM?

I have heard over the years many believers and even ministers say, "I'm tired of church!" Or "I'm tired of the mission field - I need something fresh to do in my life!" One time I heard a dear brother say when things got tough on him, "I think God is moving me from this place!" The many ideas and the foolishness that gets a hold of our minds and hearts when we don't renew ourselves in the Holy Ghost!

I heard another person say, "This type of preaching is way too basic for me, I need the deeper things of God!" If you have found yourself in this condition lately, let me help you by taking the approach of being your spiritual doctor per se.

Here is my analysis on that: When you're getting bored with "basic teaching," this is nothing more than an external sign that you have stopped hearing with your spiritual ears!" You are now cold and lifeless in the things of the Spirit. Why? No prayer life!

If there is no prayer coming from you - then there will be no renewing in the Holy Spirit for you.

THERE IS A PROGRESSION IN GOD

When one is born again, God's Spirit comes and lives within the person. He comes and makes His home in our hearts. This is the first step into the life in the Spirit. This is where you and I will understand the love of God for us and how it is God's will to live in us fully.

After we have been walking with the Lord, we can experience the infilling of the Holy Spirit. This is totally separate experience from the born-again experience. We get filled with God and begin to walk in this awesome nearness to Christ. At this point there is such an awareness of Christ in us, of sin in us and of God's holiness.

Almost at the same time, we become endued with power to be Christ's witnesses everywhere we go. We are not only seeking God's holiness for our lives but simultaneously telling the whole world about Jesus. Jesus said that we would be endued [clothed] with power from on high. Are you clothed in God's power today?

Then finally, God will release an anointing upon the vessel. If the vessel obeys God, then God's power will be manifested through the human vessel. The vessel will sense a commissioning of the Lord to go and do God's will. This anointing will come upon the vessel every time the vessel obeys God for service!

To experience just salvation or infilling, we are only experiencing a little of God. There is still endue-ment and anointing. There is so much more in God if we seek Him with all our hearts. God will draw us to Himself before He does any new work in us and through us. He will get us alone with Him and then will reveal His plan to our hearts.

Don't get bored, don't get tired or weary, no sir. Get renewed in the Holy Spirit – this is the heart of "the few."

CHALLENGE YOURSELF and GO DEEPER WITH JESUS in CHAPTER 18

1. When you think of the third person of the trinity, the Holy Spirit – what are some of His characteristics that come to your mind?

2. Have you experienced the power of God in your own life?

3. The few are a different kind of believer – they don't wait to be told what to do, they discern the wishes of the Father and act upon them.

4. Have you prayed for God to fill you with holy fire? If you have not, take some time today to pray this prayer: "Father, baptize me with your fire! Come and fill me with your holy flame of love and consume me. Break me, mold me and fill me into a vessel ready for Your use!" Amen.

5. If you find yourself getting bored, cold or confused – it's a sure sign that you need to be renewed in the Holy Spirit.

19

THE AWESOME FRAGRANCE OF JESUS

I have met quite a few believers have been under the impression that the Christian life is nothing more than a life full of bliss and blessings. They continue to add that since Jesus has already paid the debt of sin once and for all – we don't have to suffer anything in this present life.

Other believers are so caught up with the 'health and wealth' message that anything relating to carrying a cross or a life of discipline is automatically taken as some type or form of legalism.

Dear faithful, let us understand that when a man or woman submits to God to be used by Him, they must walk the path that Jesus walked. This life goes from the Garden of Gethsemane up the long and lonely walk to the cross of Calvary (without short-cuts!)

The words, **"...many are called but few are chosen...,"** rings loud and clear in my spirit.

JACOB'S VISION AND HEARTBREAK

"Then God appeared to Jacob again, when he came from Padan Aram, and blessed him. And God said to him, "Your name is Jacob; your name shall not be called Jacob anymore, but Israel shall be your name." So He called his name Israel. Also God said to him: "I am God Almighty. Be fruitful and multiply; a nation and a company of nations shall proceed from you, and kings shall come from your body. The land which I gave Abraham and Isaac I give to you; and to your descendants after you I give this land." Then God went up from him in the place where He talked with him. So Jacob set up a pillar in the place where He talked with him, a pillar of stone; and he poured a drink offering on it, and he poured oil on it. And Jacob called the name of the place where God spoke with him, Bethel. Then they journeyed from Bethel. And when there was but a little distance to go to Ephrath, Rachel labored in childbirth, and she had hard labor. Now it came to pass, when she was in hard labor, that the midwife said to her, "Do not fear; you will have this son also." And so it was, as her soul was departing (for she died), that she called his name Ben-Oni; but his father called him Benjamin. So Rachel died and was buried on the way to Ephrath (that is, Bethlehem). And Jacob set a pillar on her grave, which is the pillar of Rachel's grave to this day." (Genesis 35:9-20)

Open your spiritual ears and eyes and let us learn about this event. Jacob arrives at Padan Aram and God blesses him. His name is changed from Jacob to Israel. This typifies the spiritual progression of the believer; the believer is now advancing in spiritual maturity. His [Jacob's] character is changing and this is a wonderful thing! God tells Jacob that He is God Almighty!

It seems that before any spiritual transition begins to take full course – God impresses His Sovereignty upon the vessel he wants to use. After that, God prophesies over Israel and says, **"Be fruitful and multiply; a nation and a company of nations shall proceed from you, and kings shall come from your body. The land which I gave Abraham and Isaac I give to you; and to your descendants after you I give this land."** These were exciting times for this man and his family. God is going to use Jacob in a powerful way: **"…kings shall come from your body."**

My friends - it doesn't get more promising than for God to speak destiny into our very lives. God has a way of working destiny and purpose into our spiritual being. To all this we would be shouting, "Amen God, keep prophesying! You are so right on Lord! Amen, Amen, Amen."

The Scripture goes on to say that Jacob turned it all into a major worship service and offered worship unto the Lord with all his heart. He made it a land mark and called it Bethel: **"So Jacob set up a pillar**

in the place where He talked with him, a pillar of stone; and he poured a drink offering on it, and he poured oil on it. And Jacob called the name of the place where God spoke with him, Bethel."

How many know the joy of hearing the Lord prophesy to your heart? How many have known the awesome feeling that comes when God is talking to you through the Word or through prophetic dreams and / or visions? It's a wonderful thing! I can imagine how wonderful it must have been in the life of Jacob; but soon it was all going to change.

"Then they journeyed from Bethel. And when there was but a little distance to go to Ephrath, Rachel labored in childbirth, and she had hard labor. Now it came to pass, when she was in hard labor, that the midwife said to her, "Do not fear; you will have this son also." And so it was, as her soul was departing (for she died), that she called his name Ben-Oni; but his father called him Benjamin. So Rachel died and was buried on the way to Ephrath (that is, Bethlehem)."

As soon as the wonderful and profound words of destiny given by the Lord had filled the heart of Jacob, death came!

What a turn of events, wouldn't you say? After a beautiful time in

God's presence and the hearing of His lovely words from His very mouth – death struck! How we could mount up our complaints before the Lord and ask a million times over, "WHY GOD?" or "WHY ME?" "After all God, you gave me a word, a prophecy – this can't be happening to me now – not now!"

Beloved, a "death process" must take place for the purification of that dream, vision, or prophecy! When God brings forth new direction – death to something will immediately follow! Remember, God is changing our course – submit to His leadership!

LAY ASIDE THE HINDRACE

"Now they came to Jericho. As He went out of Jericho with His disciples and a great multitude, blind Bartimaeus, the son of Timaeus, sat by the road begging. And when he heard that it was Jesus of Nazareth, he began to cry out and say, "Jesus, Son of David, have mercy on me!" Then many warned him to be quiet; but he cried out all the more, "Son of David, have mercy on me!" So Jesus stood still and commanded him to be called. Then they called the blind man, saying to him, "Be of good cheer. Rise, He is calling you." And throwing aside his garment, he rose and came to Jesus." (Mark 10:46-50)

Before anything could have ever taken place in the life of blind Bartimaeus, he had to throw aside his garment. This garment represents our dependence on something. The garment needs go.

We cannot meet God on our own terms! It must be on His terms and only on His terms. For God to continue with His plan in the life of Jacob, Rachel had to die. It was not going to be Jacob's way; it was determined to be God's way through and through. God's vision can only be done God's way; it must be done in a way where it is God alone who gets all the glory.

THE RESULTS OF AN EXPERIENCE WITH GOD LEAVES A FRAGRANCE ON US!

After God has promised and has made everything possible to deal with His vessel, He will then fill that vessel with His fragrance.

The fragrance of Jesus, is the sweet-smelling aroma of a living sacrifice. The scent of humility, contriteness, and brokenness. This is what God is after, this is what "the few" have come to know and live to experience! Enjoy.

CHALLENGE YOURSELF and
GO DEEPER WITH JESUS in CHAPTER 19

1. Following Jesus is an impossible thing to live out in the flesh. One must come to the place of total surrender for a godly transformation to occur. Are you ready to die to self and enter in to His life?

2. Jacob typifies the carnal Christian before his life is truly broken. Have you ever been broken and made aware of your carnality and how it hinders God's plan for you?

3. As followers of Jesus, we all tend to embrace something or someone. Are you holding on to anything that can be a possible hindrance in your life and/or ministry?

4. Have you been filled with the fragrance of Jesus?

20

THE KINGDOM IS NOT FOR HALF-HEARTED PEOPLE!

"Jesus answered and said to him, "Most assuredly, I say to you, unless one is born again, he cannot see the kingdom of God." Nicodemus said to Him, "How can a man be born when he is old? Can he enter a second time into his mother's womb and be born?" Jesus answered, "Most assuredly, I say to you, unless one is born of water and the Spirit, he cannot enter the kingdom of God. That which is born of the flesh is flesh, and that which is born of the Spirit is spirit. Do not marvel that I said to you, 'You must be born again.' The wind blows where it wishes, and you hear the sound of it, but cannot tell where it comes from and where it goes. So is everyone who is born of the Spirit." (John 3:3-8)

When Nicodemus came to Jesus by night, it was with a certain motive in his heart. Nicodemus was looking for specific answers from Jesus. He had been astonished by the miracles of Jesus and had heard of the many miracles that had already taken place in the ministry of Jesus.

Nicodemus was a student of the law and teacher at that. This man knew the Old Testament Scriptures thoroughly.

There is no doubt in my mind that Nicodemus had pondered the Scriptures over and over all throughout his life; yet this man was void of understanding.

Many study the Word, but never come to the knowledge of the Truth. The Truth is a spiritual place you come into, not something you learn with your intellect.

Jesus cut to the chase and told this teacher of the Law, **"Most assuredly, I say to you, unless one is born again he cannot see the kingdom of God."** Jesus was trying to make this man understand that the ways of God were totally different than what He had been taught.

What Jesus is trying to tell Nicodemus is that, unless He would be born-again, with new eyes, new mind, new heart, new revelation, new understanding of God's Word, He would not be able to see (have perception of) the Kingdom of God.

The reason too many fall by the wayside is because they can't see the kingdom of God; they don't have spiritual vision. They don't have the right set of eyes, if you will, to see the kingdom of God - much less understand it.

Now, when a man sees Jesus and gives His life to Jesus as to follow Him wherever He goes, that servant immediately realizes that He is under marching orders. He realizes that God's Kingdom is run by Jesus Christ, He is our King! The servant of the Lord also realizes that He comes under a new government with a new set of rules to follow, etc.

Those who are truly born-again don't need explanation that their life has been brought near to God by the blood of the Lamb and are willing to serve Jesus with all their hearts – all the time!

Those who are in God's Kingdom also realizes that there are many decisions to be made which will in turn affect their spiritual and natural destiny.

For the most part, it's important for every follower of Jesus to have a heart of total surrender and submissiveness to the Holy Spirit always.

He is the One living inside the heart of the believer and has come to give all glory to Jesus. He will never lead you and me astray.

THE CROSS OF CHRIST MEANS WE WALK OUT THE LIFE OF JESUS!

"And whoever does not bear his cross and come after Me cannot be My disciple." (Luke 14:27-28)

In the plain or simple words of Jesus, He reveals to us the whole basis for effective Christian living.

He told His disciples that unless they carried their crosses and willfully followed Him, they couldn't be His disciples.

Not that Jesus was making things hard for them, but He was trying to express to them that unless they carried their crosses (this typifies the dying of the flesh, self, all ego, etc.) they would have the greatest of difficulties trying to live out this life that came from above.

We can't live out the Christian life out as prescribed in Scripture without carrying our cross and willfully following Jesus!

The believer needs to be filled and refilled with God's Holy Spirit daily if He is to make a difference with His life and be pleasing unto God.

HAS YOUR HEART BEEN CHECKED OUT LATELY?

The Holy Spirit has many ways of discovering what is truly in our hearts by the things that surround us. If we tend to be greedy, the Lord will test us in this area of money – He will make it all disappear.

If we tend to be selfish, God will test us with materialism and time. If we tend to be angry or wrathful, He will test us by taking away stuff that we love dearly.

If we a people who tend to be self-sufficient, God will "park" us in the middle of the desert and see what we do then.

I used all these examples to bring forth the truth that God loves us so much and will bring us to a place where our hearts can be tested. Not for Him to see it, but for us to see it and repent and make the necessary adjustments in our character.

Why did I entitle this message, The Kingdom Is Not for Half-Hearted People? I entitled this message like this because of the revelation God has given me regarding people who won't give Jesus their whole lives. They offer Jesus 97%, but retain 3% and convince themselves of their good deed by saying, "At least I am giving Him something!"

In the Kingdom of God, it's all or nothing! In the Kingdom of God, the half-hearted are lied to by their own minds and hearts. We think that because we have given and surrendered to God three-fourth of our lives, we are already doing God a huge favor.

Listen to what Paul said regarding the allowance of letting a little bit slip, **"You ran well. Who hindered you from obeying the truth? This persuasion does not come from Him who calls you. A little leaven leavens the whole lump."** (Galatians 5:7-9)

The Galatian believers had allowed a little bit of false teaching to come in their midst and now they were all turning back to their old religious ways.

Anytime that there is half-heartedness in us, compromise will settle in and will steal away our purpose in God. Many never really enter God's full blessing because of what I am sharing with you right now.

Here are some more examples regarding half-heartedness:

"Now it happened as they journeyed on the road, that someone said to Him, "Lord, I will follow You wherever You go." And Jesus said to him, "Foxes have holes and birds of the air have nests, but the Son of Man has nowhere to lay His head." Then He said to an-

other, "Follow Me." But he said, "Lord, let me first go and bury my father." Jesus said to him, "Let the dead bury their own dead, but you go and preach the kingdom of God." And another also said, "Lord, I will follow You, but let me first go and bid them farewell who are at my house." But Jesus said to him, "No one, having put his hand to the plow, and looking back, is fit for the kingdom of God." (Luke 9:57-62)

When I read these verses, I quickly realized that the kingdom of God is not for the half-hearted. There are many believers today who are always talking about following but that is all they ever do – they talk!

These believers get excited for God but the excitement goes as far as the church building and no further.

Others want to serve Jesus at their own convenience – it will never happen! Jesus will never use a vessel like that. Why? You are not fit! The word fit as used here in Luke 9:62 means not placed well. In other words, that vessel has not made Jesus His firm-foundation! Without that foundation, God can't use you!

CHARACTERSTICS OF A HALF-HEARTED BELIEVER

Half-hearted believers are characterized by several things. Let me share with you four things of which God has allowed me to see in my own life throughout my walk with God:

The first characteristic is fear. Half-hearted people have a disposition to fear. Fear is so controlling that it destroys the little faith that some believers have and it leaves them spiritually paralyzed for many years. They have a hard time believing that God is greater than all their needs and problems and trials. They can't see beyond their mountain of distress! Those who are bound by fear – can only see and wish. They can never carry out God's desire that burns inside them due to fear – it keeps them back.

Fear is a fruit of the flesh and only through fasting and prayer can this be broken. Once we are set free, we must go and do that thing that we have been afraid to do for so long. We must do it in the name of Jesus!

The second characteristic is doubt. Half-hearted people continually doubt if they themselves can do something for God. The problem here is pride – the focus on self to perform. Every miracle that God is going to do through you – IT'S NOT YOU! This also can only be broken by prayer and fasting. Once you give your heart to Jesus with full assurance, let Him carry you wherever He wants to take you…don't doubt the Lord. He knows exactly where to place you!

The third characteristic is guilt and shame. Half-hearted people also tend to struggle with the past. They struggle with guilt and shame. They feel that they are not good enough for God and therefore they live with this shame for years. The way that this can be broken is by understanding the awesome fact that the blood is enough! Enough to erase your past – whatever you have done! The blood of Jesus is something we believe in, not something we thoroughly understand.

The fourth characteristic is compromise. Half-hearted people have the tendency to compromise a little. They seem to think they are a little smarter than God and so they decide to barter with God on issues. They want to deal with God about kingdom business when they are talking to the King of the Kingdom.

In the Scriptures mentioned above, we found certain 'would-be' followers who never followed because it wasn't convenient.

In America, we are flooded with a spirit of apathy. People feel so lazy towards the Lord. When people compromise, they are saying to God, "Come on Lord, give us a break. We have been faithful all this time, it's about time you give us a break. People want to follow the Lord, but they want to do it their way! What happens to such a people? God passes them by! You never hear of any one of these disciples' names mentioned in Scripture. The only ones that you hear mentioned anything about are usually the one ones that went!

CHALLENGE YOURSELF and GO DEEPER WITH JESUS in CHAPTER 20

1. Have you evaluated your heart lately regarding your commitment to Jesus? Are you still following Him closely OR have you decided to follow Him from afar like some many are doing?

2. Are you walking half-heartedly after the Lord? How do you determine that you are? How do you determine that you are not? Ponder this.

3. What characteristics have you seen in your own life that you would consider as half-heartedness? Please list them and pray to the Lord to give you the strength and power to overcome them.

- _____

- _____

- _____

- _____

- _____

21

THE MARKS OF A WILLING VESSEL

"Now in the sixth month the angel Gabriel was sent by God to a city of Galilee named Nazareth, to a virgin betrothed to a man whose name was Joseph, of the house of David. The virgin's name was Mary. And having come in, the angel said to her, "Rejoice, highly favored one, the Lord is with you; blessed are you among women!" But when she saw him, she was troubled at his saying, and considered what manner of greeting this was. Then the angel said to her, "Do not be afraid, Mary, for you have found favor with God. And behold, you will conceive in your womb and bring forth a Son, and shall call His name JESUS. He will be great, and will be called the Son of the Highest; and the Lord God will give Him the throne of His father David. And He will reign over the house of Jacob forever, and of His kingdom there will be no end." Then Mary said to the angel, "How can this be, since I do not know a man?" And the angel answered and said to her, "The Holy Spirit will come upon you, and the power of the Highest will overshadow you; therefore, also, that Holy One who is to be born will be called the Son of God." (Luke 1:26-35)

When I think of a vessel for the Lord's use, I immediately think of

THE MARKS OF A WILLING VESSEL

availability, humility and brokenness. People who are vessels of the Lord are a pretty special breed that God has been building throughout time. Their lives have been through much testing and they have come forth as gold. God is now ready to consider them for His purposes!

In the story mentioned above we find God on the move one more time. He is seeking some vessel that is broken enough, shattered enough that He can fill with His glory. God chooses a humble city in Galilee named Nazareth.

Here is some brief insight into this humble city: [NAZ ah reth] (watchtower) - a town of lower Galilee where Jesus spent His boyhood years (Matt 2:23). For centuries Nazareth has been a beautifully secluded town nestled in the southernmost hills of the Lebanon Mountain rang. Situated in the territory belonging to Zebulun, the city must have been of late origin or of minor importance. It is never mentioned in the Old Testament.

However, Nazareth itself was situated in something of a basin, a high valley about 366 meters (1,200 feet) above sea level overlooking the Esdraelon valley. To the north and east were steep hills, while on the west the hills rose to an impressive 488 meters (1,600 feet). Nazareth, therefore, was somewhat secluded and isolated from nearby traffic.

This apparent isolation of Nazareth as a frontier town on the southern border of Zebulun contributed to the reputation that Nazareth was not an important part of the national and religious life of Israel. This, coupled with a rather bad reputation in morals and religion and a certain crudeness in the Galilean dialect, prompted Nathanael, when he first learned of Jesus of Nazareth, to ask, **"Can anything good come out of Nazareth?"** (John 1:46). [from Nelson's Illustrated Bible Dictionary, Copyright (c)1986, Thomas Nelson Publishers]

It is obvious that this small Galilean town was not recognized as some major city; therefore, people were not interested in its future and I'm sure that no investor would go and put all his money there to build stores and get it going as a commercial venue!

No one had this small town in view, but God! Isn't this God's economy? Isn't it for God to choose the smallest things to prove to the whole world that it is He the One who adds value to everything?

In 1 Corinthians, we find this powerful insight as Paul beautifully brings it forth when He said,

"For you see your calling, brethren, that not many wise according to the flesh, not many mighty, not many noble, are called. But God has chosen the foolish things of the world to put to shame

the wise, and God has chosen the weak things of the world to put to shame the things which are mighty; and the base things of the world and the things which are despised God has chosen, and the things which are not, to bring to nothing the things that are, that no flesh should glory in His presence." (1 Corinthians 1:26-29)

God has never been looking for glamour, talent, ability or intellect. The city of Nazareth bares this truth out when God chose it as the place for the angel Gabriel to make the most powerful declaration of the ages to Mary when he announced, **"Rejoice, highly favored one, the Lord is with you; blessed are you among women!"**

HIGHLY FAVORED ONE

I am amazed at how the Lord sees something good in us before we ourselves see it or anyone else for that matter.

When God approves something for His use, He is sure to communicate that to us. Mary was one of these vessels. She never saw the value of what she could be unto the angel Gabriel made the declaration: **"Rejoice, highly favored one!"**

Let us look more intently at this few words: The words highly favored mean to grace, i.e. endue with special honor: make accepted.

In other words, God was going to grace her with special honor; God was going to make her accepted. God was going to provide all that was necessary to carry out His function and purpose on the earth!

All you who long to be "the few" for Jesus - it is in the same manner that God looks at us and fills us with His glory. It is then that His glory is seen through us. It's all His doing. All we need is to offer ourselves completely and yield our will to His!

SOMETIMES "TROUBLE" MEANS FEAR

When the Lord wants to use you or me, He already knows about our limitations. It is with this in view that He chooses us because He knows that we will need Him to accomplish this great work He is asking us to carry out!

The angel Gabriel knew exactly what was happening when He told her that she was blessed of the Lord. Mary's reaction was typically the reaction of any person who is asked of the Lord to serve in any capacity. She was troubled! The word troubled here means, disturbed wholly.

Her whole life began to be shaken by the prophetic voice of the Lord unto her human spirit. What does this mean? It means that her disturbance was nothing more than fear! After seeing Mary's reaction, the angel said, **"Do not be afraid, Mary, for you have found favor with God."**

Two things come forth before our very eyes: fear and favor. The angel tells her not to be afraid and that the favor of God was upon her.

Oftentimes, we don't realize that if the Lord has called us to do something for Him, along with this invitation comes the favor to carry the task.

The angel was saying, "Mary, no need to be afraid; God has already found favor with You and He will take care of all the details!" Amen.

SHALL CALL HIS NAME JESUS

Anything that comes from the Spirit is spirit, and if it keeps its course – life will flow; all things that come from the flesh will remain flesh and its end will be death. The angel told Mary that the Holy Ghost would be providing all the means for Jesus to come forth!

There are several things we must realize from revisiting Mary's encounter, one of them being that everything we as believers produce, must be Holy Ghost initiated; Holy Ghost cultivated; and Holy

Ghost birthed.

The end-product will be nothing but JESUS! The fingerprints of the Holy Spirit will be all over it! You can always tell when something is not of the Lord simply by looking at the finish product. Does it have Jesus "written" all over?

WAITING FOR A RESPONSE

The characteristics of a willing vessel are not many. As a matter of fact, the characteristics are few but mostly internal in nature.

God was so willing to move through Mary. All God needed from Mary was the willingness to be used by the Creator. God was willing to release the necessary mean to accomplish this great work of giving birth to Jesus. Though God is Sovereign and Mighty in every respect of the word, He was limited to Mary's decision.

God wants to flow through us, but we need to let Him come in and dine with us. It is in this meal, in this communion time, in this intimate moment that God releases His divine nature and purpose into our hearts.

"Behold, I stand at the door and knock. If anyone hears My voice

and opens the door, I will come in to him and dine with him, and he with Me." (Revelation 3:20)

History was on hold until this crucial decision was made. After Mary heard the angel give details about how this miracle was to take place and reassuring her with, **"For with God nothing will be impossible."** Then Mary said, **"Behold the maidservant of the Lord! Let it be to me according to your word." And the angel departed from her."** (Luke 1:37-38)

Once the response is given to God, all heaven begins to move! As soon as we choose to follow in obedience to God, the Lord reinforces our decision by performing awesome signs and wonders on our behalf.

ARE YOU PREGNANT WITH GOD?

Will we be the carriers of His purposes on the earth? Will we be expressions of His divine nature here on earth? Will we allow Him to impregnate our hearts with Jesus or more of Jesus?

Will we surrender our spiritual wombs to give fresh declarations of Jesus the Son of God in the last days?

I believe the Holy Ghost is presently moving in the hearts of those listening. It may not be the "feels like the right thing to do," but we must set our feelings aside and pursue the will of God to its fullest.

May we be found by our Lord – willing!

CHALLENGE YOURSELF and
GO DEEPER WITH JESUS in CHAPTER 21

1. Have you ever considered that God is looking at you with favor and that He longs to use you to make the difference in this world?

2. What is your interpretation of 1 Corinthians 1:26 - 29? What does it mean to you personally?

3. Fear only stays so long as faith is absent! Once you begin to "walk out" God's plan – fear leaves!

4. Has God given you a specific calling to follow? Has it come to fruition yet? If not, maybe God is still waiting for your response!

5. Are you pregnant with God? Is there a vision God has placed inside your spiritual womb?

22

TURNED INTO ANOTHER MAN

"Then Samuel took a flask of oil and poured it on his head, and kissed him and said: 'Is it not because the LORD has anointed you commander over His inheritance? When you have departed from me today, you will find two men by Rachel's tomb in the territory of Benjamin at Zelzah; and they will say to you, 'The donkeys which you went to look for have been found. And now your father has ceased caring about the donkeys and is worrying about you, saying, "What shall I do about my son?"' Then you shall go on forward from there and come to the terebinth tree of Tabor. There three men going up to God at Bethel will meet you, one carrying three young goats, another carrying three loaves of bread, and another carrying a skin of wine. And they will greet you and give you two loaves of bread, which you shall receive from their hands. After that you shall come to the hill of God where the Philistine garrison is. And it will happen, when you have come there to the city, that you will meet a group of prophets coming down from the high place with a stringed instrument, a tambourine, a flute, and a harp before them; and they will be prophesying.Then the Spirit of the LORD will come upon you, and you will prophesy with them and be turned into another man. And let it be, when these signs

come to you, that you do as the occasion demands; for God is with you." (1 Samuel 10:1-7)

Turned into another Man is a message that "the few" have come to understand as the touch of God upon them - a consecration that one must have if they are to be useful for God.

In the passage above, we find the Prophet Samuel on a mission from God – to anoint the first king of Israel.

"Now the LORD had told Samuel in his ear the day before Saul came, saying, "Tomorrow about this time I will send you a man from the land of Benjamin, and you shall anoint him commander over My people Israel, that he may save My people from the hand of the Philistines; for I have looked upon My people, because their cry has come to Me." So when Samuel saw Saul, the LORD said to him, "There he is, the man of whom I spoke to you. This one shall reign over My people." (1 Samuel 9:15-17)

As Saul begins to talk to the Seer (Samuel), God begins to prophesy through him. God begins to unveil specific directions for Saul and Samuel tells him, **"Then the Spirit of the Lord will come upon you, and you will prophesy with them and be turned into another man."**

There is no doubt in my mind that when God calls out a man for His work, God equips the servant for the task ahead of him! One other thing that is evident of a man that has been touched of God is the fact that the breath of God comes upon Him with power and is felt every time He delivers for God.

Now it is interesting to make a quick study on the word turned. This man was to become something other than what He was. Saul was going to experience a touch of God that would empower and enable Him "**… to do as the occasion demands."**

The word turned as used in 1 Samuel 10:6 comes from the original Hebrew word haphak (haw-fak'); a primitive root; to turn about or over; by implication, to change, overturn, return, pervert. In the King James Version, it is used as become, change, come, be converted, give, make [a bed], overthrow (-turn), perverse, retire, tumble, turn (again, aside, back, to the contrary, every way).

Saul was to become a man totally changed from what He was. The Spirit would come upon Him and change him. He would become a champion according to some translations. God would touch Him with His Spirit and Saul would become a champion for God. Glory to Jesus for His awesome anointing upon our lives!

Please understand that when God chooses a vessel for Himself, He will go to great lengths to prepare Him, but not without anointing it first!

TURNED INTO ANOTHER MAN

As followers of Jesus and servants of God, the few, understand to some degree how this works.

God chooses us for specific purposes and anoints us for the task ahead. There was no way God was going to use Saul in his old ways. God needed to touch this man with His Spirit and enable him to think like God, walk like God and lead like God!

The need to be so filled with God has never been greater than it has been in these times we are presently living today.

When we talk about being 'turned into another man' we are not just talking about nice little feelings and goose bumps. When we deal with this work of God, we are dealing with the mind, the heart and the Spirit.

First, let us deal with the mind. Our mind is and will continue to be the battle ground in our lives. An un-regenerated mind has the potential to hinder God. A mind that has not been given over to the Lord will cause great delays regarding the purposes of God, not to mention fears and doubts regarding His will.

The Apostle Paul reminds the church in Corinth about the mind of Christ: **"These things we also speak, not in words which man's wisdom teaches but which the Holy Spirit teaches, comparing spiritual things with spiritual. But the natural man does not receive the things of the Spirit of God, for they are foolishness to him; nor can he know them, because they are spiritually discerned. But he who is spiritual judges all things, yet he himself is rightly judged by no one. For "who has known the mind of the LORD that he may instruct Him?" But we have the mind of Christ."** (1 Corinthians 2:13-16)

The mind of Christ has been given so we can discern the things that God is trying to communicate to us who live on earth. He has left us the ability to navigate through life with confidence. It is the mind of Christ that we need today.

Secondly, He has turned our hearts around. Our hearts were so given to selfishness. Our hearts were so possessed by our fleshly desires – no wonder God changes our hearts. Listen to the prophecy regarding a new heart: **"For I will take you from among the nations,** gather you out of all countries, and bring you into your own land. Then I will sprinkle clean water on you, and you shall be clean; I will cleanse you from all your filthiness and from all your idols. I will give you a new heart and put a new spirit within you; I will take the heart of stone out of your flesh and give you a heart of flesh. I will put My Spirit within you and cause you to walk in My statutes, and you will keep My judgments and do them." (Ezekiel 36:24-28)

The need for a new heart is not just a nice idea, but a great need if we are going to do the will of the Lord.

We must be willing to let God have all our hearts – we must let Him possess us totally!

In the Acts of the Apostles, the Scripture laid out by Luke has powerful insight: **"And when He had removed him, He raised up for them David as king, to whom also He gave testimony and said, 'I have found David the son of Jesse, a man after My own heart, who will do all My will.' From this man's seed, according to the promise, God raised up for Israel a Savior — Jesus."** (Acts 13:22-24)

The Scripture says that David understood the heart of God! David was possessed with the idea that God was everything to Him. God knew David as a man after His own heart! David longed for the heart of God. He was consumed in knowing God's emotions!

It is impossible for a man to understand the heart of God if a man is not willing to be broken by God! Unless a man is turned into another man (and that not by his own will but by the touch of God,) he will never learn the heart of God!

The spirit of man must be awakened and set ablaze for God's glory! One of the things that must happen in God's servant is to have an encounter with the glory of God. The glory of God must be so impressed in a vessel before He can be turned into another man.

Having "casual" experiences with God don't really do anything. It is when the glory of God is impressed upon the inner man that we become God possessed. Every time that God comes to touch us with His glory it is with the intent to change us. The impression of His glory can only be consummated by our immediate obedience to this touch.

HOW WE ARE CHANGED

We have discussed in some length the need to be "turned into another man" and how Saul was touched by God. Let us look at how the

Apostle Paul teaches us that 'change of heart' takes place: **"I have been crucified with Christ; it is no longer I who live, but Christ lives in me; and the life which I now live in the flesh I live by faith in the Son of God, who loved me and gave Himself for me."** (Galatians 2:20)

If we are to enter the fullness of God's design for His creation and endeavor to fulfill His purposes here on earth, we [our flesh] must be totally removed from the picture. It is impossible to live for God if we don't crucify our old nature.

Jesus said, **"If anyone comes to Me and does not hate his father and mother, wife and children, brothers and sisters, yes, and his own life also, he cannot be My disciple. And whoever does not bear his cross and come after Me cannot be My disciple."** (Luke 14:26-28)

Our Lord teaches us that we can't be His disciples if we don't carry the cross. The cross is nothing more and nothing less than our dying place. We must live lives that are dead to self, so Christ can be exalted. The only way to

follow Him is if our lives are cancelled out! The cross will make sure that our lives are dead and gone and that the life of Christ is activated in us.

The only way that change takes place, yes, the only way that we are turned into another man is by way of the cross.

WHY DO WE NEED TO BE CHANGED?

We must be changed for the sake of the work of God. Unless we are changed we won't be able to do it God's way! The work of God is such a delicate issue that only those who are 'turned into another man' can really carry it forth.

To try living out the Christian life or to even try doing God's work in the flesh is a total set up for failure and disapproval. God has wishes and desires for His creation; He also has much to share with them. The only way that we can get in tune with God is if we are turned into another man.

CHALLENGE YOURSELF and
GO DEEPER WITH JESUS in CHAPTER 22

1. Have you heard the cry of the Lord for you to go forth in His Name?

2. Have you experienced God's anointing for your calling?

3. When you think of being "changed into another man," what is the first things that come to your mind?

4. Paul said in Galatians 2:20 that he had been crucified with Christ… Have you been crucified with Christ?

23

UNBELIEF BEINGS GOD'S GREATEST OBSTACLE
Part 1

"Now it came to pass, when Jesus had finished these parables, that He departed from there. When He had come to His own country, He taught them in their synagogue, so that they were astonished and said, "Where did this Man get this wisdom and these mighty works? Is this not the carpenter's son? Is not His mother called Mary? And His brothers James, Joses, Simon, and Judas? And His sisters, are they not all with us? Where then did this Man get all these things?" So they were offended at Him. But Jesus said to them, "A prophet is not without honor except in his own country and in his own house." Now He did not do many mighty works there because of their unbelief." (Matthew 13:53-58)

Not too long ago I came across a quote that impacted my soul in a very deep way. The quote was made by a man of God named Leonard Ravenhill. The quote reads like this: "We must cease the opportunity of a lifetime during the lifetime of the opportunity!" What does this mean? It means that there are "spiritual" windows and doors of opportunity that open for us during our lifetime.

How we interpret opportunities can bring powerful results in our lives, whether for good or for bad! I believe that that these windows and doors present themselves every time God is getting ready to start a new "season" or "chapter" in our spiritual journey.

A WINDOW OF OPPORTUNITY OPENED IN NAZARETH

The Scripture that I used as our text will outline much of the revelation that God desires from "the few."

After Jesus had taught the multitudes many parables He departed from them and came to His own country and taught them in their synagogue.

The Lord who is full of mercy showed up in His own country to bring revival to those who were spiritually dead and indifferent.

The Lord began to reveal Himself as a teacher and it was so powerful that the people were astonished by His teaching and wisdom, "... **He taught them in their synagogue, so that they were astonished and said, "Where did this Man get this wisdom and these mighty works?"**

Not only was Jesus moving in wisdom but mighty works were also taking place. No wonder the people were astonished.

Let us look at the word astonished. The word astonished in the Greek is *ekplesso* which means **to strike with astonishment**. The King James Version translates it **amaze**. The people were amazed at Jesus and the mighty works He was performing. Can you imagine the emotional rush felt by those who were present?

I wonder how many of those present remember any word from the sermon on that day; or how many on that day were stirred to follow Jesus with a full-hearted devotion?

Dear members of "the few," a window of opportunity had opened to all who were present; a window that guaranteed the wisdom, power, and life everlasting in God. It was a window of opportunity that would get many of them over the hump of traditional religiosity and ritualism. It was a window of opportunity that carried much purpose and destiny.

Oh, servant of God! Jesus was there and His power was available and even human excitement (emotion) was present to make this cross-over or pass through this window of opportunity even more possible; but sadly, only a few were transformed.

The same thing happens today in churches across the world: the music is moving to the beat of the Holy Spirit, yes to the heartbeat of heaven, Jesus manifests His presence, tongues, interpretations and prophecies begin to flow amid the congregation - but nothing changes!

Oh, what amazement! We are "wowed" time and time again – our minds are convinced, our emotions are convinced, but our hearts sit in a tomb of unbelief!

We walk out of the church with just words of how great the service was but we are not changed! Isn't this sad? Isn't this grieving to the Holy Ghost? Externally, it's all there; but internally, we are missing what God is trying to say.

UNBELIEF IS THE STENCH OF FLESH!

As soon as faith was beginning to come forth in the lives of these hearers from the Nazarene Synagogue (as Jesus spoke and performed mighty works,) the flesh stuck its ugly head and began to doubt Jesus! Isn't this the pattern in most believers? Much spiritual movement, but no spiritual response to go with it!

One should wonder why is it that with all the godly preaching, the many bibles, commentaries, tapes, CD's, etc., we find ourselves powerless when it comes to touching society.

Our churches are filled with compromisers who won't carry a cross and will get easily offended when a preacher tells them to "turn or burn!" People come to God and get "amazed" but won't lay down their lives to believe His Word! They place their lives above Christ's life!

These types of believers are carrying an anti-Christ spirit in their very hearts: **"Let no one deceive you by any means; for that Day will not come unless the falling away comes first, and the man of sin is revealed, the son of perdition, who opposes and exalts himself above all that is called God or that is worshiped, so that he sits as God in the temple of God, showing himself that he is God."** (2 Thessalonians 2:3-4)

As soon as the amazement set in, unbelief followed. That is why I am so down on fleshly amazement or astonishment. Those types of emotions need to be monitored and kept in check in our spirit.

Please notice: as soon as the "sense of happiness" settled in, they began to question in their hearts. Just listen to the kind of questions they were asking themselves: **"Is this not the carpenter's son? Is not His mother called Mary? And His brothers James, Joses, Simon,** and Judas? And His sisters, are they not all with us? Where then did this Man get all these things?" So they were offended at Him." The flesh has many characteristics when it tends to rebel against the Lord's doing. It manifests itself in many forms but nothing is more wicked that trying to make Jesus Christ just like us – of pure human descent!

Though Jesus was one-hundred percent God and one-hundred percent man, He was still born from above. He was conceived by the Holy Ghost. No flesh was involved in His conception.

"Then the angel said to her, "Do not be afraid, Mary, for you have found favor with God. And behold, you will conceive in your womb and bring forth a Son, and shall call His name JESUS. He will be great, and will be called the Son of the Highest; and the Lord God will give Him the throne of His father David. And He will reign over the house of Jacob forever, and of His kingdom there will be no end." Then Mary said to the angel, "How can this be, since I do not know a man?" And the angel answered and said to her, "The Holy Spirit will come upon you, and the power of the Highest will overshadow you; therefore, also, that Holy One who is to be born will be called the Son of God." (Luke 1:30-35)

The flesh hates Jesus! In hates to obey Jesus! That is why those who were amazed at His words at first were quickly swayed by their human intellect [flesh] and started making Jesus of the earth. **"Isn't He the carpenter's son? Is not His mother Mary? And His brothers James, Joses, Simon, and Judas? And His sisters, are they not all with us?"**

This is the way that many believers are robbed from entering in and passing through this "window of opportunity!" They hear about what God can do and even see what God can do for themselves, but they soon doubt and their hearts are full of unbelief and miss out on the richness that Christ can bring to their lives.

UNBELIEF WILL ROB THE BELIEVERS FROM HIS PURPOSE AND DESTINY

"But Jesus said to them, "A prophet is not without honor except in his own country and in his own house." Now He did not do many mighty works there because of their unbelief."

After the service was over, Jesus left with little success. Though people were amazed and though people were "amen-ing" every word He spoke, they never appropriated His words into their very hearts. Unbelief took over and the results were sad, very sad!

The Scripture goes on to say that **"...He did not do many mighty works there because of their unbelief."**
Do you see this? Unbelief in the heart will keep anybody out of God's plan and purpose not to mention destiny!

What is this unbelief? The original word in Greek is apaistia (ap-is-tee'-ah) faithlessness. It means that the people were astonished in their emotions, but in their hearts, they discredited everything that Jesus said and did. They were in a state of faithlessness. In other words, they were without faith.

HUMILITY IS THE PLATFORM WHERE FAITH STANDS

Faith comes through humility and acknowledging that God is everything and must be everything. When a man believes Jesus, He immediately knows that He cannot live that life on His own power or by His own emotions....so what does He do? The man must humble himself and ask for God to help him live this life out. Here's a passage that brings this out: **"And when He came to the disciples, He saw a great multitude around them, and scribes disputing with them. Immediately, when they saw Him, all the people were greatly amazed, and running to Him, greeted Him. And He asked the scribes, "What are you discussing with them?" Then one of the crowd answered and said, "Teacher, I brought You my** son, who has a mute spirit. And wherever it seizes him, it throws him down; he foams at the mouth, gnashes his teeth, and becomes rigid. So I spoke to Your disciples, that they should cast it out, but they could not." He answered him and said, "O faithless generation, how long shall I be with you? How long shall I bear with you? Bring him to Me." Then they brought him to Him. And when he saw Him, immediately the spirit convulsed him, and he fell on the ground and wallowed, foaming at the mouth. So He asked his father, "How long has this been happening to him?" And he said, "From childhood. And often he has thrown him both into the fire and into the water to destroy him. But if You can do anything, have compassion on us and help us." Jesus said to him, "If you can believe, all things are possible to him who believes." (Mark 9:14-23)

Please understand that a man can only find faith as he or she positions himself by humbling their hearts before the King of Kings. The secret of men and women of God and how they conquered mountains for Jesus is found in the secret chambers of humility! It was until they realized that Jesus was in charge that their lives began to be used for the glory of God.

Remember, it's all about Jesus getting all the glory; and when a weak human vessel begins to shine, it's not because of his flesh but because of the glory of God that has filled him!

CHALLENGE YOURSELF and
GO DEEPER WITH JESUS in CHAPTER 23

1. Meditate on this:

    a. Have you ever felt like you missed some valuable opportunities in your walk with the Lord?

    b. Do you recall the reason(s) you passed them by?

    c. What did you learn from not taking the opportunity?

    d. Have you had another opportunity to make up the for the one you didn't take?

24

UNBELIEF BEING GOD'S GREATEST OBSTACLE
Part 2

"Today, if you will hear His voice: "Do not harden your hearts, as in the rebellion, as in the day of trial in the wilderness, when your fathers tested Me; they tried Me, though they saw My work. For forty years I was grieved with that generation, and said, 'It is a people who go astray in their hearts, and they do not know My ways.' So I swore in My wrath, 'They shall not enter My rest.'" (Psalm 95:7-11)

"Beware, brethren, lest there be in any of you an evil heart of unbelief in departing from the living God; but exhort one another daily, while it is called "Today," lest any of you be hardened through the deceitfulness of sin. For we have become partakers of Christ if we hold the beginning of our confidence steadfast to the end, while it is said: "Today, if you will hear His voice, do not harden your hearts as in the rebellion." For who, having heard, rebelled? Indeed, was it not all who came out of Egypt, led by Moses? Now with whom was He angry forty years? Was it not with those who sinned, whose corpses fell in the wilderness? And to whom did He swear that they would not enter His rest, but to those who did

not obey? So we see that they could not enter in because of unbelief." (Hebrews 3:12-19)

I want to begin today by saying that unbelief has been the greatest obstacle in the human heart. Unbelief is a sin of the flesh! Unbelief defies God and makes God's Word a mockery. People who walk in unbelief today are mockers of God and His Word.

Whenever unbelief shows up, God doesn't manifest Himself there. If Jesus comes in, then unbelief must go. It can't be that both are in operation in the human heart. We must learn to yield to God's voice and God's holy Word.

Walking in the higher realm of commitment with Christ, joining "the few," unbelief must be eradicated from your heart. Faith must be the only economy a servant of Jesus comes under.

OUR MAKER

"Oh come, let us worship and bow down; let us kneel before the LORD our Maker. For He is our God, and we are the people of His pasture, and the sheep of His hand." (Psalm 95:6-7)

If we are going to become people of faith, we must have it very clear in our hearts that God oversees our lives. We are not our own. He bought us with a price and we belong to Him.

A person who walks in faith believes that God is who He said He was. If the Lord was to confront one of us, would we be ready to respond to Him and say, "I believe in You wholeheartedly and everything You tell me is for me!"

The Lord is our Maker; He knows us better than we know ourselves. He understands our fears, doubts, and struggles. He knows that if we make the right decision regarding His Word, He will reinforce our decision. If we as believers keep following our minds, then we will more than likely disobey Him and miss out on God's best for us.

Many believers today live on "morsels of yesterday." We are walking with the Lord on an experience that was so great yesterday, but haven't received any fresh revelation as of late due to our disobedience. We haven't moved up one inch with God because He is no longer entrusting us with fresh bread from heaven. It is God's desire that we obey Him so He can continue "making or fashioning" us into His likeness. Remember He is our Maker.

HEARING HIS VOICE CARRIES RESPONSIBILITY

Every time that the Lord speaks to us in a personal way, He does it so it can produce change in us. If the Lord spoke something to us, we are responsible to carry it out! If we don't carry out His Word, we disobey and we won't be changed - thus the lack of maturity in our lives. How many can relate to this?

The children of Israel were tested in the wilderness for the sake of transformation. God's plan was to make His people a people of faith. By doing this, He would be able lead them through the wilderness and bring them over the Jordan into the land that flowed with milk and honey.

Obviously, the children of Israel were anxious to get to the Promised Land, but wanted nothing to do with obedience. This sounds like many believers today: They want the religion but no accountability; they want salvation without a cross; they want the institution but no strings attached; they want God's blessings but without condition!

The Scripture as written in the Psalm bears out a most terrifying consequence spear-headed by unbelief. Listen to the Holy Ghost warning: **"Today, if you will hear His voice: "Do not harden your hearts, as in the rebellion, as in the day of trial in the wilderness, when your fathers tested Me; they tried Me, though they saw My work. For forty years I was grieved with that generation, and said,**

'It is a people who go astray in their hearts, and they do not know My ways.' So I swore in My wrath, 'They shall not enter My rest.'"

The Holy Ghost makes this word applicable for today, not yesterday. He is saying that if "Today," we hear His voice we should not harden our hearts as our forefathers did when they were tried. They became rebellious to the voice of God and due to their rebellion forfeited the "rest" that God had for them.

Do you know why so many believers today live confused lives? Most of it can be attributed to rebellion against a Holy God. The Holy Spirit commanded them to make a change here or there, or to simply just trust but they didn't bow before the Word of the Lord and consequently are now living a life of "un-rest!"

The Lord puts us in a wilderness so He can test us. After His Word goes forth to our hearts during our trial, He waits for our decision. Nothing will be said anymore until a decision is made.

I believe that here's about the time that we begin to call people and look for some sympathy somewhere – but God will not move until a decision is made. By the time, we start asking someone for their opinion, in our heart of hearts, we already know what we need to do in the sight of God. If we follow what our spirit is telling us, we will find rest.

IN GOD, BELIEVERS NEVER FAIL A TEST, THEY JUST KEEP RETAKING IT UNTIL HE PASSES IT!

I believe the Lord is patient and kind. I believe the Lord understands what we go through and therefore releases His compassion and megaton love upon us. But I also understand that there are some lessons that God has for me that will help me get to the place of rest.

The tests in God are not made to destroy me, but to draw me closer to Him. They are made with the most tender touch and with spiritual advancement in mind. The Lord wants to promote my life into a richer and deeper relationship with Him. He wants me to learn to continually bask in His presence, to take hold of His garment daily. His tests are simply to make me one that will put Him first above all things.

THE SECRET OF DISCIPLINE

"Beware, brethren, lest there be in any of you an evil heart of unbelief in departing from the living God..." (Hebrews 3:12.)

We have already read on how our forefathers forfeited their blessing due to the sin of unbelief. I believe the Holy Ghost is calling afresh to a renewed walk of faith in Him.

In God, we either obey or disobey – there is no middle ground. There is no let me think it through. We must learn the secret of discipline. The secret of discipline is being quick to hear and quick to obey!

Whenever the Lord tells us to do something, we must act on it at once. It is vital that we learn this principle in our life with God.

To depart from the living God means to have a heart of unbelief. You might say, "But Pastor David, I really love Jesus! But I can't trust Him. I can't trust Him with my family, job, money, future, etc."

Once you see Christ, it's not a matter of trust but obedience! The sinner who hasn't met Jesus is still trying to decide if he can trust God, but we who are saved, we know we can bank/trust on Him. So, for us [who believe] it is not a matter of trust, but obedience!

A VISITATION FROM THE LORD

The Promised Land was a type or shadow of the real thing. The rest that the Scripture talks about is none other than Jesus Himself. Amen. As we become obedient to Him, we begin to see Him as He really is – then we began to be changed into His likeness.

To love the Lord and to obey Him is the greatest reward here on earth. A visitation from the Lord should be the most satisfying thing that will happen to a believer before he sees Jesus face to face.

"Jesus answered and said to him, "If anyone loves Me, he will keep My word; and My Father will love him, and We will come to him and make Our home with him." (John 14:23)

For those who long to be obedient to the Lord in all things, get ready, for the Father and Jesus will come and make their home [to stay, abide, continue, dwell, endure, be present, remain] with you!

Are we ready to move on with God and start experiencing the high calling of God in Christ Jesus? Are we willing to invite Him to speak knowing that we will take full responsibility for the words that He speaks to us? Are we ready to enter His rest or for Him to enter His rest in our hearts? Selah.

CHALLENGE YOURSELF and
GO DEEPER WITH JESUS in CHAPTER 24

1. Our relationship with God pretty much determines the degree of our obedience whether we will follow or not. Is your relationship with the Lord deeper this year than it was last year?

2. Every time God speaks to our hearts through the Holy Spirit, we are responsible to carry out the revelation. Have you obeyed the last thing God told you to do?

3. Did you know that in God you won't fail a test – you will simply just keep retaking it until you pass it! When were you last tested by God? What was the test? Did you advance?

25

UNBELIEF BEING GOD'S GREATEST OBSTACLE
Part 3

GOD'S PROPHETIC WORD MUST COME FORTH FIRST, BEFORE ANY EFFECTIVE MOVEMENT CAN BE MADE.

"And the LORD spoke to Moses, saying, "Send men to spy out the land of Canaan, which I am giving to the children of Israel; from each tribe of their fathers you shall send a man, everyone a leader among them." "Then Moses sent them to spy out the land of Canaan, and said to them, "Go up this way into the South, and go up to the mountains, and see what the land is like: whether the people who dwell in it are strong or weak, few or many; whether the land they dwell in is good or bad; whether the cities they inhabit are like camps or strongholds; whether the land is rich or poor; and whether there are forests there or not. Be of good courage. And bring some of the fruit of the land." Now the time was the season of the first ripe grapes. So they went up and spied out the land from the Wilderness of Zin as far as Rehob, near the entrance of Hamath. And they went up through the South and came to Hebron; Ahiman, Sheshai, and Talmai, the descendants of Anak, were there. (Now Hebron was built seven years before Zoan in Egypt.) Then

they came to the Valley of Eshcol, and there cut down a branch with one cluster of grapes; they carried it between two of them on a pole. They also brought some of the pomegranates and figs. The place was called the Valley of Eshcol, because of the cluster which the men of Israel cut down there. And they returned from spying out the land after forty days." (Numbers 13:1-2, 17-25)

It seems very interesting to me to see how the Lord guides and directs His children. God never asks us to do anything that He is not willing to back-up. He never makes decisions for us when it comes down to our obedience, but He will always re-enforce our decision.

God's plan was simple (as it always is when He is in charge!). God's plan from the beginning was to bring His people to a place that flowed with milk and honey. It was God's longing for His people to enter a time of great prosperity and divine provision. It was God's intent to establish His people forever as "the people of God."

As always, God works through His people. God gets His will accomplished on the earth through the obedience of His children. This seems to be the most powerful of ways throughout Scripture that God demonstrated His mighty deeds – through His servants, "the few."

The children of Israel had come to a place once again in deciding to follow the Lord, but this time, it was into the land of Promise. This should have been enough to make everybody rejoice! This was to be the greatest of moments in the history of the Hebrew children.

The Lord spoke to Moses and said to him, **"Send men to spy out the land of Canaan, which I am giving to the children of Israel…"** This was going to be the final test before God's children would enter in. Up to this point, God had been patient with the rebellious children of Jacob. He had put up with much indifference and was giving a last test. This was the test of tests if you will.

WHY DOES GOD INVITE US TO SEE THE PROMISE FIRST, BEFORE HE GIVES IT TO US?

I've always wondered why God gives us precious promises or prophetic dreams and visions, or simply just a revelation out of Scripture regarding our futures and then doesn't fulfill them right there and then?

I believe that this historic account of the children of Israel in the book of Numbers will unfold this (sometimes) overwhelming question or uncertainty.

I honestly believe that the Lord allows us to see the beauty of a promise and its fulfillment for several reasons.

The first reason we can see the promise, is so that faith can be imparted into our human spirit. It is when we see with our spiritual eyes what God has in store that we first learn to "cling" to the Lord and be patient for His "word" to be fulfilled in us as it is written, **"... that you do not become sluggish, but imitate those who through faith and patience inherit the promises."** (Hebrews 6:12)

We don't get faith by working at it; we get faith by waiting on God.

The second reason we are shown the promise is so we can realize our lack of power to conquer anything in the flesh! God never called us to do anything for Him in our own strength. We can surely try doing that, but we will get burned out and become drained emotionally and physically.

IT WAS GOD'S DESIRE, NOT MAN'S - TO POSSES THE LAND!

"Now they departed and came back to Moses and Aaron and all the congregation of the children of Israel in the Wilderness of Paran, at Kadesh; they brought back word to them and to all the congregation, and showed them the fruit of the land. Then they

told him, and said: "We went to the land where you sent us. It truly flows with milk and honey, and this is its fruit. Nevertheless the people who dwell in the land are strong; the cities are fortified and very large; moreover we saw the descendants of Anak there. The Amalekites dwell in the land of the South; the Hittites, the Jebusites, and the Amorites dwell in the mountains; and the Canaanites dwell by the sea and along the banks of the Jordan." (Numbers 13:26-29)

"But the men who had gone up with him said, "We are not able to go up against the people, for they are stronger than we." And they gave the children of Israel a bad report of the land which they had spied out, saying, "The land through which we have gone as spies is a land that devours its inhabitants, and all the people whom we saw in it are men of great stature. There we saw the giants (the descendants of Anak came from the giants); and we like grasshoppers in our own sight, and so we were in their sight." (Numbers 13:31-33)

After God had promised them a land that flowed with milk and honey, he commissioned Moses to send out twelve spies (these represent leadership). It was God's desire for His people to enter this long-awaited blessing.

The servants of the Lord went with God's hand upon them to spy out this land and to bring forth a report of their findings.

At some point during their venture - what was to be God's plan became man's burden. Man started making that which was heavenly into something earthly. Man started to feel that it was their responsibility to bring forth God's dream in their own way. This can be overwhelming if you know what I mean.

Dear members of "the few," this is something we continue doing in our walk with Christ even today!

Jesus gives us a prophetic word or promise for some future time and we start figuring out methods and begin strategizing different means (not to mention the putting of a time frame) on this promise to be fulfilled.

The Lord's promises are to be done by Him and Him alone. God doesn't give us all kinds of insight so we can break our heads in trying to figure out how it is to be carried out or accomplished.

The grave error that the children of Israel committed was that they took this vision of God and made it their own personal responsibility instead of leaning on the Lord's arm to bring it to pass as He had done in previous times.

Is it any wonder that their hearts were gripped with fear when they saw the giants of Anak there? Isn't it any wonder that many believers today fail in their lives or endeavors – all because they take what is of God away from His hands and place the promise upon their own hands?

I can't stress this point enough: The children of Israel failed to see that it was God's dream for them; they quickly forgot that it was God's dream not theirs! God's dream can only be done God's way and in God's time!

CALEB AND JOSHUA – MEN OF A DIFFERENT SPIRIT

"Then Caleb quieted the people before Moses, and said, "Let us go up at once and take possession, for we are well able to overcome it." (Numbers 13:30)

"But Joshua the son of Nun and Caleb the son of Jephunneh, who were among those who had spied out the land, tore their clothes; and they spoke to all the congregation of the children of Israel, saying: "The land we passed through to spy out is an exceedingly good land. If the LORD delights in us, then He will bring us into this land and give it to us, 'a land which flows with milk and honey.' Only do not rebel against the LORD, nor fear the people of the land, for they are our bread; their protection has departed from them, and the LORD is with us. Do not fear them."** (Numbers 14:6-10)

Of all the people who came out of Egypt from that first generation, Caleb and Joshua had a heart to follow the Lord wholly.

These servants of the Lord didn't give in to their carnal desires and made God's plan something of the earth. They were firm in believing that that which God had promised He was also able to perform. Joshua and Caleb thought the same way, they were filled with God's faith and understood that it wasn't their battle but God's.

THE LORD TAKES DELIGHT ON THOSE WHO DELIGHT IN HIM.

"If the LORD delights in us, then He will bring us into this land and give it to us, 'a land which flows with milk and honey.'" (Numbers 14:8)

Caleb and Joshua obviously delighted (chaphets [Heb.] - to delight in, to take pleasure in, to desire, to be pleased with) in the Lord's command. In other words, God's command was enough for them to believe. They didn't need some prop or some gimmick to believe God's word.

Caleb and Joshua understood that the only thing they needed to do was to obey what they had heard! God's word was enough to bring them through every obstacle that would stand in their way!

There was no "giant" big enough in the known world that would scared these two men of God – these men with a different spirit, these members of "the few!"

CHALLENGE YOURSELF and
GO DEEPER WITH JESUS in CHAPTER 25

1. Can you recall the last time that God was challenging you to take a step of faith and how difficult it was? Share your experience.

2. It is one thing to do something you want to do; it is totally another thing to do what God wants you to do. Keep your spiritual ears and eyes open to God's voice always!

3. God will show us His vision for a thing and then release the faith so we can walk in it. Are you still waiting patiently for your vision to come to pass? Are you finding it difficult to wait upon the Lord for it?

4. God has great plans for you and I. The only thing is that we must move on it in His timing and with His wisdom. This can be a real test. Take time to study God's ways of accomplishing miracles in the Old and New Testament.

5. Caleb and Joshua were men of a different spirit. God commended them for being a company of faithful servants – are you a faithful servant?

MINISTRY INFORMATION

For more information regarding the ministry of Masterbuilder Ministries, Inc., preaching engagements, leadership training or conferences, School of Ministry - feel free to email David Mayorga:

david_mayorga@sbcglobal.net
mayorga1126@gmail.com

Also, check out our website at:
www.masterbuildertx.com

Our ministry can be located at:

**Masterbuilder Ministreis, Inc.
3833 N. Tauylro Rd.
Palmmhurst, Texas 78573**

MINISTRY RESOURCES

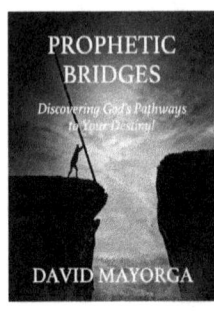

Prophetic Bridges
by David Mayorga

ISBN *978-17333174-5-0*

Inextinguishable!
by David Mayorga

ISBN *978-0-9991710-8-0*

The Value of the Elements
by David Mayorga

ISBN *978-0-999171-0-4*

ALL BOOKS CAN BE
PURCHASED THROUGH

SHABAR PUBLICATIONS

www.shabarpublications.com

www.ingramcontent.com/pod-product-compliance
Lightning Source LLC
Chambersburg PA
CBHW070558300426
44113CB00010B/1312